DATE DUE

march	10 -03	IL:263	1979
DEC 1 3 2006			

Demco, Inc 38-293

The Measurement and Development of Empathy in Nursing

WILLIAM J. REYNOLDS
University of Stirling

Ashgate

Aldershot • Burlington USA • Singapore • Sydney

Published by
Ashgate Publishing Ltd
Gower House
Croft Road
Aldershot
Hants GU11 3HR
England

Ashgate Publishing Company
131 Main Street
Burlington
Vermont 05401
USA

Ashgate website: http://www.ashgate.com

British Library Cataloguing in Publication Data
Reynolds, William J.
    The measurement and development of empathy in nursing. -
    (Developments in nursing and health care)
    1.Nurse and patient 2.Empathy
    I.Title
    610.7'30699

Library of Congress Control Number: 00-131252

ISBN 0 7546 1264 3

Printed and bound in Great Britain by MPG Books Ltd, Bodmin, Cornwall

Contents

List of Tables

List of Figures

Foreword

Empathy as an essential component of all helping relationships forms the focus of this significant publication. The author, using his considerable clinical, research and teaching experience and expertise, sets out a framework for the teaching and evaluation of empathy together with a reliable and valid assessment instrument to establish the level and nature of practitioner empathy. It is unusual to find this combination of empirically based guidance contained in a single text.

Empathy is recognised as a fundamental aspect of all helping relationships and has been the subject of many scholarly discussion papers, particularly in recent years. However, it still presents as a problematic and challenging phenomenon for practitioners, researchers and educationalists alike. In an attempt to better understand this phenomenon numerous questions have been asked. For example, is empathy an innate or acquired quality? Is it largely an emotional, cognitive or behavioural process? Are certain personality types more likely to have it than others are? Is it present in all types of interpersonal interaction?

Based on evidence, this text can provide certain tentative answers to some of the above questions as illustrated by the outcomes of the empathy education programme. This would suggest that it is possible to teach at least something of an empathic response. Although some questions may be answered the author raises a number of challenges for nurse teachers about the nature of students' educational experience and how education may impact on the students' potential to promote both the personal growth of their clients and that of themselves.

It has been clearly stated by many writers that empathy encompasses such concepts as respect, warmth, trust, understanding and genuineness. Also reinforced is that the quality of an empathic relationship is about understanding another individual during their period of distress.

Therapeutic relationships form the basis of all helping interventions and not just those carried out by nurses. Embedded within such relationships are social, emotional and behavioural elements, all of which are given attention within this text

Emphasis is given to the relationship process and what takes place between the client and the practitioner. Importantly, noting that during a therapeutic intervention the practitioner must understand the nature of the client's distress and be able to manage the situation with skill, confidence and sensitivity. A therapeutic relationship demands more than merely reflecting back to the client what is being said or to offer an evaluation. The practitioner must be able to journey alongside the client to get inside the shoes of the person, to gain a sense of what it feels like to be that person and be able to convey such sentiments to the person by way of thought and deed.

So much of this process is based on the intangible or the invisible. A position which has been problematic for many health care professionals, but particularly nursing as intangibles, cannot be measured. Hitherto, this lack of measurement has meant that much of what nursing does at an interpersonal level has not attained the same overt credibility as the more tangible aspects. The assessment tool described in this work can contribute to the articulation and disentanglement of the core process elements and make the intangible more tangible. In turn this will help make it possible to identify, quantify and evaluate more accurately the contribution of nursing to health care, an important feature in the current economic and evidence-based culture.

Emphasised throughout the text is the importance of learning from the experience of doing. Whilst learning from simulation and role-play is valued greater importance is given to working with clients in the clinical environment. Given that the author is drawing on his extensive experience as practitioner, researcher and teacher and well able to get into the shoes of all three groups, this provides absolute credibility to the genesis of the text. This credibility is further enhanced as the evidence reported has been accumulated from working in partnership with students, teachers, practitioners and researchers.

This work is an extremely valuable contribution to the existing contemporary knowledge base. Although intended primarily for the nursing profession it has much wider application across the caring sciences.

Professor Mary Chambers, D. Phil, RN
University of Ulster

Preface

Empathy is known to be crucial to helping relationships. The problem is that professional helpers, including nurses, do not normally display it. A major reason for this is that empathy has not been measured in clients' terms and accordingly taught. The low level of empathy can have negative consequences for clients. This book reports a study in which a reliable and valid client-centred empathy scale has been developed. The scale is based on an operational definition of empathy that is relevant to clinical nursing. Using this scale, a course has been designed and implemented which does help nurses to learn how to show empathy. Nurses' gains in empathy persisted for some time (3-6 months) after the course had finished. Such a course may help others to learn as well.

The major aims of this study were: i) the development and evaluation of the empathy scale, ii) the investigation of variables that may affect nurses' ability to offer empathy, and iii) the evaluation of the empathy course. The findings of this study have implications for the future design of nurse education and the goals of the health service. The relevance of the findings to the goals of the health service are indicated by the suggestion in the Patient's Charter that clinicians need to collaborate with users of health services in the prioritising of clinical needs and the setting of treatment goals.

Bill Reynolds, PhD., MPhil., RN.
Reader in Nursing
University of Stirling
Highland Campus
Inverness

Acknowledgements

The ongoing assistance and support of Professor Janet Grant is gratefully acknowledged. I would also like to acknowledge the loving support from my wife, Margaret, my daughter, Iona, and my cat, Tizer.

1 Empathy is crucial to helping

The literature reviewed in this chapter substantiates the widely held view that empathy is crucial to all forms of helping relationships. Additionally, while there is confusion about whether empathy is a personality dimension, an experienced emotion, or an observable skill, it is shown that empathy involves an ability to communicate an understanding of a client's world. Finally, the definition of empathy used in this study is introduced. This definition is relevant to the goals of clinical nursing, which include the need to understand clients' distress, and to provide supportive interpersonal communication.

1.1 Why empathy is crucial to helping

In this section, it will be shown that:
a)   empathy is crucial to all helpful interpersonal relationships;
b)   the purpose of helping relationships is emphasised by a definition of the helping relationship cited in this section;
c)   the purpose includes: i) the development of a safe interpersonal climate and, ii) to enable clients to cope more effectively with threats to their health;
d)   several studies indicate that empathy enables professionals to appreciate the client's perspective and to respond in ways that result in favourable outcomes for those seeking help.

An extensive argument can be found in the literature to support the view that helper empathy is an important facilitator of constructive interpersonal relationships. While referring to the helping relationship in the contexts of clinical psychology, nursing, and medicine, Truax (1970) emphasised that without empathy there is no basis for helping. This view has been repeated by many other writers. Thus Kalish (1971) wrote:

> a voluminous amount of the accumulated research and theoretical findings on interpersonal relationships supports the idea that

> empathy is the most critical ingredient of the helping relationship
> (p 202)

and Carver and Hughes (1990) (in the context of intensive care units):

> the sterility of a mechanical (high technology) environment makes
> the caring, comforting functions of professionals critically
> important, yet difficult to achieve. Technical competence is
> necessary, but must be combined with interpersonal skills such as
> empathy, warmth and respect, before the patient feels health
> professionals care (p 15).

1.1.1 The purpose of the helping relationship

To consider the implications of the available research evidence supporting
the hypothesised relationship between empathy and helping, it is useful to
review the intended outcomes of the helping relationship. Irrespective of
whether the helping process is referred to as counselling (Anthony, 1971),
psychotherapy (Truax and Mitchell, 1971), human relations (Gazda et al.
1984), therapeutic relationships (Kalkman, 1967), interpersonal relations
(Peplau, 1988), teaching (Chambers, 1990), or simply caring (Watson,
1985), all writers refer to similar aims or purposes. These include: i)
initiating supportive interpersonal communication in order to understand
the perceptions and needs of the other person, ii) empowering the other
person to learn, or cope more effectively with their environment, and iii)
the reduction or resolution of the problems of another person.

Kalkman (1967) who refers to the helping relationship as
relationship therapy, provided an operational definition of the nurse-client
relationship which includes aims and purposes that are likely to be
common to all helping disciplines. She states that:

> relationship therapy refers to a prolonged relationship between a
> nurse-therapist and a patient, during which the patient can feel
> accepted as a person of worth, feels free to express himself without
> fear or rejection or censure, and enables him to learn more
> satisfactory and productive patterns of behaviour (Kalkman, 1967,
> p 226).

Kalkman's (1967) definition of the helping relationship is congruent with those provided by numerous other theorists (eg. Peplau, 1952; Rogers, 1957; Ashworth, 1980; Wilson and Kneisl, 1983; La Monica, 1987). This definition provides a useful basis for commenting on the research concerned with the efficacy of empathy in the interpersonal process. A review of the literature suggests that there are considerable grounds for accepting the view that empathy is a critical variable in determining the outcomes postulated by Kalkman. While the available research evidence is not necessarily conclusive, numerous contributors to the literature on interpersonal relations have found it persuasive.

1.1.2 The importance of a supportive interpersonal climate

Kalkman (1967) states:

> relationship therapy refers to a prolonged relationship between a nurse therapist and a patient, during which the patient can feel accepted as a person of worth, and feels free to express himself without fear of rejection or censure... (p 226).

In relation to this view, several studies have suggested that empathy can help create an interpersonal climate that is free of defensiveness and that enables individuals to talk about their perceptions of need. The difficulty in drawing firm conclusions from these studies is partly related to the fact that researchers have measured empathy differently. While most studies have defined empathy in a cognitive-behavioural way, the use of different measures means that the construct being measured among studies is not necessarily the same. A review of a sample of the available studies emphasises this point.

A study by Mitchell and Berenson (1970) viewed empathy in a cognitive-behavioural way, as operationalised by the Truax Accurate Empathy Scale. With respect to confrontation of unpleasant or maladaptive behaviour, these researchers found that during the first counselling session, highly-empathic therapists, significantly more than low-empathy therapists, used approaches which provided important information about the therapist, focused on the here-and-now relationship between therapist and client, and emphasised the client's resources. On the other hand, low-empathisers were more likely to confront clients with pathology rather than with their resources.

A study by Reynolds (1986) reported that as clients' ratings of student-nurse empathy increased among repeated measures on the Empathy Construct Rating Scale (La Monica, 1981), their anecdotal descriptions of the students' behaviour during a series of counselling interviews suggested that they felt more able to be open with their student. Typical examples included: *"It's hard for her to understand me, but she is trying very hard"* (second counselling interview), *"I can talk freely to her, there is no barrier"* (fifth counselling interview).

While there is a danger that clients might say what they think that people want to hear, the specific nature of clients' comments suggested that they experienced sensitive understanding from the students and became less defensive. In spite of the possible limitations arising from social desirability factors, these data encourage the idea that trust was developing in the relationship as a consequence of nurses' attempts to understand their clients.

Howard (1975) interviewed clients in several clinical settings in order to investigate the conditions perceived to be necessary for humane care. Analysis of the interviews, observation of nurse-client interactions and the literature on personalised care led Howard to identify cognitive - behavioural empathy as a necessary variable for humane care. Howard reported that empathy helps professionals respond to clients as unique human beings because they can see the world from the vantage point of their client, and better understand and respond to their needs.

Lyon-Halaris (1979), commenting on non-verbal behaviour, reported that low-empathy nurses mainly exhibited listening via non-verbal behaviour, for example, avoidance of eye contact, eyebrows down, wrinkled forehead and the crossing and uncrossing of legs. High-empathy nurses were also reported to laugh significantly less than low-empathy nurses. Following the interviews, clients completed the Barrett-Lennard Relationship Inventory (Barrett-Lennard, 1962), a client measure of cognitive-behavioural empathy, rating the degree of empathy they felt from nurses. An analysis of variance determined high and low-empathy nurses ($p<.05$); 3 nurses were highly empathic and 2 were not. The researcher then compared the frequency and duration of non-verbal behaviours for high and low-empathy nurses. While differences were found between high and low empathisers in terms of non-verbal behaviour, the only significant findings from a test of the difference in mean frequency related to laughter (p<.02) and leg movements (p<.01).

A limitation of this study is the small sample (n = 5). However, it is of interest because the client sample reported that the non-verbal behaviours of low empathisers tended to convey a lack of respect, interest and support. Interest and support seem similar to Rogers' (1957) concept of warmth. Absence of commitment from the helping person is likely to interfere with the development of trust in the helping relationship. To trust another person with personal information requires that the client believes that the information will only be used for the purpose for which it was given (Ritter, 1994). Absence of trust is likely to act as a barrier to empathy because it is less likely that a client will be open and sharing with information.

The creation of an initial interpersonal "climate" that is free of defensiveness would seem highly desirable in view of the fact that health professionals have the arduous task of conveying emotionally charged information to the public. Fear, anger and misconception lead some professionals to respond in a discriminatory manner to clients with socially undesirable problems (see Haines, 1987). These issues include problems of family violence, child abuse, wife battering and abuse of the elderly. Group self-help approaches recommended by Petit (1981) and Valenti (1986) have been demonstrated to require empathic skills to encourage sharing and openness among group members.

1.1.3 Empathy and therapeutic outcomes

Kalkman's (1967) description of the helping relationship also suggests that it is a purposeful activity which has as its final objective, client growth. She states that:

> relationship therapy...enables the client to learn more satisfactory and productive patterns of behaviour (p 266).

Several studies have supported the hypothesised relationship between empathy and favourable health outcomes for clients.

Feital (1968) pointed out that numerous studies have established a correlation between empathy, the helping relationship, and measures of outcomes such as improved health or more effective learning. Truax and Mitchell (1971) cite more than a dozen studies supporting their belief that empathy is a major determinant of successful outcomes for clients in counselling and psychotherapeutic situations. Rogers (1975) reiterated once again his belief in the crucial role of the empathic process when the other person is 'hurting'. He summarised a sample of 22 research findings that support his belief.

Since Rogers' (1975) paper, the research evidence has accumulated, and studies have supported the view that empathy is a primary ingredient in helping relationships (eg. Gladstein, 1977; Coffman, 1981; Altman, 1983; McKay et al., 1990). However, the nature of inquiry is one in which facts are not treated as self-evident givens (Schwab, 1962), and some studies showing conflicting results suggest that the debate has not yet ended (eg. Hart, 1960; Sloane et al., 1975; Rocher, 1977; Newall, 1980).

At best it can be said that the majority of the studies conducted over the past four decades have supported the hypothesised relationship between empathy and the ability to help another person. In nearly all cases empathy has been conceptualised in a cognitive-behavioural manner, relying on client-reports or ratings by objective judges.

The results reported so far are congruent with many other studies. For example, Siegal (1972) found improvement among children with learning disabilities in both verbal and behavioural spheres related to time in play therapy, and therapists' levels of empathy, warmth and genuineness. Additionally, Kendall and Wilcox (1980) demonstrated a significant relationship between empathy and therapist effectiveness during their treatment of hyperactive and uncontrolled children.

Evidence that empathy may be a more important facilitator of a helpful relationship than the helper's ideological orientation came from a study by Miller et al. (1980). This study found that behaviour therapists who scored high in empathy, were more potent reinforcers of adaptive behaviour than therapists who were low empathisers.

In his later years, Rogers extended his theory of client-centered psychotherapy to other situations such an encounter groups and play therapy. He also became interested in the application of his theory to education and extended it to interpersonal relations in general (eg. Rogers, 1960 and 1977). This resulted in empathy research extending into the student-teacher relationship. For example, a study by Aspey (1965) found that in three classes where the teacher's empathy was highest, the pupils showed a significantly greater gain in their reading achievement than in those classes with a lesser degree of that quality. These findings were consistent with an enlarged study be Aspey and Roebuck (1975) that extended for more than a decade. The evidence that they accumulated suggests that the attitudinal climate of the learning environment, as created by the teacher, is a major factor in promoting or inhibiting learning (Hughes and Huckill, 1982).

The role of empathy in the helping process requires further investigation against specific outcome criteria. However, in spite of the conflicting results among studies, the specific positive effects of empathy upon the needs of helpers remains a reasonable proposition. This is of interest to nurse educators because of the widely accepted view that empathy is crucial to effective interpersonal processes and essential at the onset of a relationship (eg. Mitchell and Berenson, 1970; Gazda et al. 1975; La Monica et al. 1987; McKay et al. 1990; Graham, 1993). Further research evidence is commented on in Chapter 2 that supports the need for empathy in clinical nursing.

1.2 The meaning and components of empathy

In this section, it will be shown that:

a) there is a debate around empathy as a personality dimension, an experienced emotion, or an observable skill;

b) empathy needs to involve the client's actual awareness of the helper's communication in order that clients know whether they are being understood;

c) accurate empathy is a form of interaction, involving communication of the helper's attitudes and communication of the helper's understanding of the client's world;

The need to find a common definition of empathy is emphasised by the disagreement in the literature about what empathy means. Empathy has been variously conceptualised as: i) a behaviour, ii) a personality dimension, and iii) an experienced emotion (McKay, 1990). During the past decade, several writers (eg. Davies, 1983; Williams, 1990; Morse et al. 1992; Bennett, 1995) have suggested that as a result of the complexity of the empathic process, confusion exists about the meaning and components of empathy. These writers propose that empathy is a multidimensional, multiphase construct which is often considered in a narrow way as a unitary construct.

Following an extensive review of the literature, Morse et al. (1992) identified four components of empathy: moral, emotive, cognitive and behavioural (see Figure 1).

Figure 1: Morse's components of empathy

Component	Definition
Emotive	The ability to subjectively experience and share in another's psychological state or intrinsic feelings
Moral	An internal altruistic force that motivates the practice of empathy
Cognitive	The helper's intellectual ability to identify and understand another person's feelings and perspective from an objective stance
Behavioural	Communicative response to convey understanding of another's perspective

Similarly, Williams (1990) informs us that the most widely recognised components of empathy are emotional empathy, cognitive empathy, communicative empathy, and relational empathy. The additional component of relational empathy was defined as experienced or client-perceived empathy. Williams' conclusion, which did not involve moral empathy, was broadly similar to Patterson's (1974) earlier definition of empathy.

Patterson (1974) described empathy as involving four concepts or stages. Firstly the helper must be receptive to another's communication, the emotive or moral component. Secondly, the helper must understand the communication by putting himself in the other's place, the cognitive component. Thirdly, the helper must communicate that understanding to the client, the behavioural or communicative component. Finally,

Patterson suggested that empathy allowed for the possibility of the client validating the helper's perception of the client's world, a relational component.

The additional component of relational empathy is arguably an outcome that is dependent on and related to the helper's cognitive and behavioural/ communicative ability, in order that the client may be offered the opportunity to validate the helper's perceptions, and to experience being understood. The client's actual awareness of the helper's communication allows him/her to say, "Yes that is how I see things" and, "Yes that is what I would like to happen". This assumption is consistent with Barrett-Lennard's (1981) multidimensional model of empathy. That writer referred to his model as the empathy cycle, describing it in the following manner:

Phase 1. The inner process of empathic listening to another who is personally expressive in some way, reasoning, and understanding;

Phase 2. An attempt to convey empathic understanding to the other person's experiences;

Phase 3. The client's actual reception/awareness of the helper's communication.

When the process continues, Phase 1 is again the core feature, and 2 and 3 follow in cyclical mode. The total interactive sequence within which these phases occur begins with one person being self-expressive in the presence of an empathically attending other, and this characteristically leads to further personal expression and feedback to the empathising partner.

The different components of empathy identified by Morse et al. (1992) among others, from their thorough review of the literature, may all contribute to empathy but the extent to which they are all interrelated appears to be a source of disagreement among theorists. This seems particularly so in respect of the extent to which all components are necessary, or contribute to behaviours that build therapeutic, problem-solving relationships.

In spite of frequent references to empathy as a human quality emphasising moral, emotive, and cognitive qualities, alternative views can be found in the literature. Several theorists have conceptualised empathy in a manner which emphasises its cognitive-behavioural components. Thus Truax (1961) wrote:

> accurate empathy involves more than just the ability of the therapist to sense the client's "private world" as if it were his own. It also involves more than just the ability of the therapist to know what the client means. Accurate empathy involves the sensitivity of current feelings and the verbal facility to communicate this understanding in a language attuned to the client's feelings. (p 2).

The Truax definition emphasises that empathy is a way of perceiving, as well as a way of communicating. It has shifted the emphasis from a trait or human quality to a form of interaction. This definition of empathy would also appear to be congruent with the cognitive and behavioural components of empathy alluded to by Morse et al. (1992).

Similarly, Rogers (1975) who tended to view empathy as an attitude emphasised the communicative aspect of the construct. He suggested that the facilitative conditions operative in all effective relationships relate to the helper's attitude, cognition and behaviour. Rogers argues that the client learns to change when the helper communicates commitment (warmth) and non-defensiveness (genuineness), and is successful in communicating understanding of the client's current feelings (empathic). Later, Rogers (1990) repeated his view that the attitudes and cognitive ability of the helper are conveyed to the client through the communication of the helper. This suggests that when attitudes and understanding are shown to the client, empathy is a skilled behaviour.

Following the Truax definition of empathy, there has been an increasing tendency among theorists (eg. Zoske et al., 1983) to argue that empathy is an interpersonal concept, comprising a specific set of interpersonal or communication skills, rather than being an instinctive quality possessed by certain persons. Empathy has increasingly been viewed in a cognitive-behavioural way and described as a skill and an ability (Morse, 1994; Jaffrey, 1995). For example, Aspey (1975) sees empathy as:

.. the ability to communicate your understanding of the   other person's feelings and the reasons for his feelings (p 11).

Similarly, Valle (1981) states that:

> empathy is the ability to respond to the feelings and reasons for the feelings the patient is experiencing in a manner that communicates an understanding of the patient (p 784).

1.3 The definition of empathy used in this study

In this section, it will be shown that:

a)   there is a need for a definition of empathy that reflects what the literature says that nurses should be doing during clinical work;

b)   the definition of empathy used in this study involves communicating understanding of the client's experience in order that this can be validated by the client.

Since the focus of this study is concerned with the ability of nurses to offer empathy, there was a need for a definition of empathy which reflected the communication skills of nurses. The definition of empathy subscribed to here, and used in the research reported later in this thesis, is that of La Monica (1981):

> empathy signifies a central focus and feeling with and in the client's world. It involves accurate perception of the client's world by the helper, communication of this understanding to the client, and the client's perception of the helper's understanding. (p 398).

The definition includes perceptual and interactional empathy, it is a cognitive-behavioural definition. It combines the two levels of empathic attitude and communicative ability. In this context empathy is not only a "way of being" with another (Rogers, 1975) but it also communicates to clients the professional's understanding of their world so that this perception can be validated by the client.

Further interest in this definition stemmed from the researcher's conclusion that it reflected what the literature said that nurses should be doing during relationships with their clients (Storch, 1982; Hamilton, 1982; MacKay et al., 1990). This includes initiating supportive interpersonal communication with persons who are in need of affective support, in order to understand their distress, and appreciate what it is like to be in the client's position. The relevance of this to nursing is that several writers (eg. Gordon et al. 1980; Tschudin, 1982; Kickbush and Hatch, 1983) have suggested that nurses need to allow clients to have a more active role in problem-solving, especially concerning their needs for practical and emotional support. It was concluded that the definition provided a starting point for understanding the construct of empathy within nursing practice. The relevance of La Monica's definition of empathy to clinical nursing is discussed further in Chapter 2.

1.4 Summary of the need for empathy

Conclusions drawn from the literature reviewed in this chapter are that:

a)   empathy is crucial to a non-defensive relationship;
b)   empathy can facilitate satisfactory and productive outcomes for clients and other recipients of helping relationships.

The conclusions drawn from the literature suggest also that empathy is an interpersonal skill that is dependent upon the attitudes and behaviours of the helping person. Empathy is a form of interaction, involving communication of the helper's attitudes, and communication of the helper's understanding of the client's world. It involves the client's actual awareness of the helper's communication in order that clients know whether they are being understood. While empathy contains many components, it is an observable skill. However, there is a need for a common understanding of what is meant by empathy.

Since the cumulative research evidence supports the assumption that empathy is a crucial component of a helping relationship, there is a need to find an operational definition of the concept that is relevant to clinical nursing. The definition of empathy offered in this chapter appears to be relevant to what nurses ought to be doing during relationships with their clients. It involves an accurate perception of the client's world and an ability to communicate this understanding to the client, in order that the client is aware of the nurse's perception of the client's position. The relevance of empathy to clinical nursing, and the extent to which nurses offer empathy to clients, is considered in Chapter 2.

2 The problem: Professional helpers, including nurses, do not normally display much empathy

This chapter examines some of the observations that motivated this study. Firstly, while empathy is crucial to all helping relationships, professional helpers do not generally offer much empathy. Secondly, while nurses are meant to provide helping relationships, they do not normally show much empathy to clients. The relevance of empathy to clinical nursing and the potential consequences of low-empathy nursing for clients is considered.

2.1 General problem: Professional helpers do not normally display much empathy

In this section, it will be shown that:

a)   a low level of empathy has been reported among the helping professions;
b)   this indicates that many professional helpers are not as helpful as they ought to be.

Unfortunately it has been shown in the literature that the ability to offer empathy is lacking among professionals in the helping professions. Carkhuff and Berenson (1967) stressed that those individuals in our society designated as 'more knowing', e.g. teachers, ministers, nurses, doctors and psychologists, have often created feelings of impotence among recipients of their help. The low level of empathy offered in professional relationships has been reported in numerous studies and widely commented on in the literature.

Keatochvii et al. (1967) used a five-point measure of empathic ability, where a score of 3 indicated minimal ability to understand another person. These researchers reported that senior psychology and education students (future professionals) functioned just below level 2. At this level, they are almost completely unaware of the feelings and experiences of the other person. The same findings were reported by Carkhuff et al. (1967) and Martin and Carkhuff (1968) who investigated the empathic ability of experienced guidance counsellors and psychotherapists.

Since these findings, several contributors to the literature have reported that many helping professionals are unable to demonstrate empathy at a level necessary to understand the concerns of the client. For example, Christiansen (1977) reported low levels of empathy among occupational therapy students, Disiker et al. (1981) observed a decline in medical students' empathy scores over time, Hills and Knowles (1983) reported that nurses actually blocked clients' expressions by changing the subject, and Sloane (1993) reported that many physicians sampled became defensive, and withdrew from the client. Further examples include Squier (1990) who reported that a study of doctors' interpersonal skills demonstrated a tendency by subjects to dominate clinical interviews and ask for factual information, rather than listen to clients and reflect their feelings. Later Wheeler and Barrett (1994) reported that a sample of nurse educators were generally low in empathy.

While referring to the low levels of empathy among helping professions, Kalish (1971) expressed the view that:

> The tremendous lack of human nourishment in the everyday
> life environment of people is appalling. (p 202).

This problem was alluded to by Squier (1990) in relation to health care when he expressed concern that practitioner - client relationships were not accorded more priority alongside technological advances. He suggested that a possible explanation is that practitioners do not know what processes in their relationships with clients are responsible for ultimate therapeutic benefit for those who are suffering or experiencing crisis situations. This possibility is supported by Williams' (1992) observation that hospital systems seem conducive to flattening the humanity of its employees. This writer pointed out that staff too can experience crisis when they feel vulnerable, sad and exposed during professional relationships, because they may be experiencing aspects of life that are unfamiliar to them. This situation would appear to require empathic support from a senior colleague. However, Williams (1992) has questioned the extent to which clinical staff experience a relationship where fears, concerns and worries can be openly discussed.

The concern about the low level of empathy reported in professional relationships is that the recipients of help may not perceive that their situation is understood. It is difficult to understand how a helping person can assist the other person to meet their needs unless they possess an ability to offer an empathised awareness of what the other person wants to happen, or is experiencing.

For example, in relation to teaching, it seems necessary that a teacher can understand what a learner has already learned, and how the learner feels about learning, in order to offer experiences necessary to promote further learning (Rogers, 1969; Bandura, 1977). For this reason, the low level of empathy observed in education students, guidance counsellors and nurse educators should be a concern.

In relation to health care, Squier (1990) states that in the fields of chronic illness, long-term and stress related illness, an empathic relationship between the client and practitioner may mean the difference between misery, suffering and pain and a relatively active, satisfactory and productive life. For this reason, the low level of empathy observed in psychologists, nurses, occupational therapists and doctors should be a concern. Since research shows a positive relationship between professional empathy and outcome, the low level of empathy reported across all professions indicates that many professional helpers are not as helpful as they ought to be.

2.1.1 Summary of the general problem

In this section, it has been shown that many professional helpers are unable to offer empathy at a level necessary for understanding the recipient of help. Because the helping professions exist in order to help people, it is essential that professionals communicate attitudes of caring and an empathised awareness of the other person's situation. The literature reviewed in this section substantiates the view that many recipients of professional help may not feel that their situation is understood by professionals.

2.2 Specific problem: Nurses do not normally display much empathy

In this section, it will be shown that:

a) although empathy is important to the goals of clinical nursing and the achievement of favourable outcomes for clients, nurses have been found to show low levels of empathy;

b) a concern about the low levels of empathy in nursing is that it can have negative consequences for clients.

2.2.1 The relevance of empathy to clinical nursing

Carver and Hughes (1990) provided an extensive rationale for the place of empathy in nursing. They propose that empathy is crucial to the nurse's involvement with changing health demands arising from increased technology, different health/illness patterns in the management of chronic and terminal care, and the rise of consumerism. The proliferation of technology in some health-care environments requires that nurses humanise care. Chronic illness requires that nurses assist clients to modify and manage their living conditions, and make major emotional adjustments. Since nursing involves a series of relationships with significant others, clients, families and colleagues in the health team, empathy could be considered to be an essential pre-requisite for effective nursing practice, and ultimately of fulfilling a variety of nursing goals. These goals relate to the clinical and educational aspirations of the profession. Examination of these goals provides a specific basis for defending the contribution of empathy to clinical excellence in nursing.

  It has long been argued in the nursing literature that the nurse-client relationship is the 'cornerstone' of all care delivered (e.g. Kalkman, 1967; Ashworth, 1980; Faulkner, 1985; Chambers, 1990). All writers suggest that it has the potential to influence positive health outcomes for clients. For example, Ashworth (1980) proposed that the four main aims of nurse-client communication were:

a) to develop a relationship in which clients perceived the nurse as being friendly, competent, reliable and helpful and as appreciating the client's individuality and worth;

b) to establish clients' needs as seen by them;

c) to provide information which can be used by clients to structure their expectations;

d) to assist clients to use their individual resources and those made available to them.

If the aims of the nurse - client relationship are not achieved there are likely to be problems. It is unlikely that clients will be able to trust nurses if they do not view them as being helpful and appreciative of their individuality. If nurses fail to establish clients' needs as seen by them it is unlikely that they will be able to understand the clients' responses to health problems objectively, or address the clients' needs. Failure to provide needed information may mean that clients view nurses as omnipotent experts who lack commitment to them. Finally, if nurses do not assist clients to use their individual resources, clients may not be able to achieve optimum health. The concerns expressed here are discussed further in the remaining part of this section.

An important aim of the nurse - client relationship is to understand what the client needs from nurses and to assist the client to take charge of their own life (Carver and Hughes, 1990). In order to make an assessment of need, a nurse needs to hear what the client is saying, and then validate the inferred meaning of this with the client. Orlando (1972) proposed that this ability leads to the identification of the client's perception of need and paves the way for mutual planning of interventions relevant to the resolution of the client's problems.

2.2.1.1 Establishing an interpersonal climate for nursing assessment
Establishing clients' needs as seen by them is likely to be dependent in part upon the clients' capacity to feel safe within their relationships with nurses. Unless clients are able to trust nurses in an open two-way relationship, it is unlikely that nurses will be able to assess accurately the needs and problems of their clients from a client-centred viewpoint.

Truax and Carkhuff (1967) proposed that trust has its origins in certain facilitative conditions offered by the helper. These conditions were identified as warmth and genuineness which involved commitment to helping, openness and consistency. Carkhuff and Truax stated that these conditions are of central importance to any trusting relationship, and have an interlocking nature with empathy. For example, it is unlikely that trust can occur unless clients experience a prior or concomitant feeling of warmth or genuineness.

Kreigh and Perko (1979) operationally define trust as being a belief in self and others. They further suggest that it is an outgrowth of a feeling of security. This is likely to be critical to the reduction of feelings of insecurity that may result from daily living problems or more complex covert and unexpressed concerns of clients about threats to their health

(Baillie, 1995). Unless nurses are able to reduce clients' feelings of insecurity by demonstrating openness and commitment it is unlikely that clients will be able to share their perceptions of their experiences.

Collins (1983) highlights a further issue relating to trust and empathy. He suggests that when a relationship has not reached a stage of mutual trust, more may be gained in the long term if the client's state of readiness is respected. Pushing a client into revealing what he/she is not ready to discuss can be harmful. This may result in the intensification of the anxiety which might exist as a consequence of health problem(s), or maladaptive living patterns. If this happens it will be a problem because severe anxiety can result in loss of control and impaired problem-solving ability (Peplau, 1990; Barry, 1996).

Judging when to ask questions about the client's health or coping patterns is a strategic therapeutic decision. According to Collins (1983) timing of interventions is dependent upon an empathised awareness of the client's state of readiness. That awareness must be achieved during the initial stages of a new nurse-client relationship. According to Collins, if this is not achieved, it is less likely that clients will talk eventually about events that are important to them. Peplau (1990) has pointed out that anything that is not talked about, merely acted out, is less likely to be understood by the nurse or the client.

In conclusion, trust provides an interpersonal climate where it is possible for clients to talk about their perceptions of need. This provides nurses with the opportunity to make an assessment of need which is critical to the practice of nursing (Roy, 1980). However, clients' abilities to talk about their perceptions of need is dependent on a nurse-client relationship that has the characteristics of a non-threatening relationship.

2.2.1.2 Understanding clients' responses to health problems objectively
The development of an interpersonal climate that enables clients to talk about their perceptions of need is crucial, but not sufficient. A further issue relating to the goals of clinical nursing is the extent to which nurses understand objectively the origins and purposes of clients' responses to health problems. Several writers (Roy, 1980; Auger and Dee, 1982; Peplau, 1990) have suggested that this implies that nursing assessment involves more than naming or labelling a problem. It includes

understanding how a person attempts to maintain his health. This involves understanding empathically the goal of the client. The goal is defined as what the client wanted to happen when he adopted a particular coping response to an actual or perceived threat to his health.

If empathy is absent, it will be a real problem because the nurse's ability to help the client to learn how to cope effectively with life stressors will be reduced. This is indicated by suggestions in the literature that people appraise a situation based upon what is important to them, their vulnerabilities, goals, coping styles and capacities (Lazarus et al., 1984; Kim et al., 1993). Examples of coping styles may include denial, alcohol abuse, hostility and avoidance of a situation. The possible goals of such responses to health threats may include the need to avoid anxiety, loneliness and embarrassment. Unless nurses possess an empathised awareness of the client's goals and capacities, it is unlikely that the nurse can provide care that is appropriate to the client's needs.

Roper et al. (1990) stated that as a therapeutic nurse-client relationship develops, more information will be volunteered about the client's subjective perception of the need and coping. This seems relevant to the planning and implementing phases of the nursing process. However Rogers (1961) points out that the resolution of dysfunctional coping requires an ability to listen to the feelings behind the client's words. The response is likely to be dependent on the helper's ability to be reflective, roughly analogous to cognitive empathy, and determined by the helper's objectivity. Truax and Carkhuff (1967) stated that genuineness implies an openness to the experience of the other person, a tendency to be non-judgmental.

According to Rogers (1961) a barrier to the exploration of feelings is the very natural tendency to judge, evaluate or disapprove, when a client's communication is ambiguous or personally threatening. He suggests that when this happens helpers can become defensive, often transmitting this to the client through unwanted advice, failure to respond to direct questions, or curt unfriendly voice tone. Rogers and Truax (1966) proposed that the logical means of correcting this tendency is to work on achieving genuineness. This suggest that once this is established, the work of helping proceeds through the helper's moment-by-moment empathic grasp of the meaning and significance of the client's world.

The research evidence supporting the need for empathy in helping relationships has been reviewed in Chapter 1. The studies cited in the next section provide support for the view that high empathy nursing can result in favourable health outcomes for clients.

2.2.2 *The need for empathy in clinical nursing*

Several nursing studies give preliminary evidence that the nurse's use of empathy is likely to make a difference to client outcomes. Gerrard (1978) showed a positive relationship between Rogers' (1957) core interpersonal conditions and client responses. Such responses included relief from pain, improved pulse and respiratory rates, and clients' report of reduced worry and anxiety. This outcome is somewhat congruent with Dawson's (1985) report that clients with hypertension were different from other clients. They perceived less empathy in clinicians, and attributed greater importance to discussing with their health care provider their responses to health care, as compared with personal problems and lifestyle matters.

Since clients in Dawson's (1985) study expressed a need to discuss their responses to health care, nurses need to demonstrate commitment to listening to such clients. Otherwise, an opportunity for clients to have an active role in problem-solving will be lost and nurses will fail to appreciate clients' individuality.

Williams (1979) studied the effects of empathy in the nursing care of the institutionalised elderly to determine if empathy might reduce the dehumanisation and depersonalisation of the client's environment, as measured by changes in self-concept. Nurses offered low and high levels of empathy to elderly clients over an eight-week period. A statistically significant increase in the self-concept of clients experiencing high empathy was demonstrated. Peplau (1990) suggests that adequate self-concept act as an anti-anxiety device and results in more satisfactory relationships with significant others.

Williams' (1979) findings support the view expressed earlier that warmth and genuineness have an interlocking nature with empathy. A major source of improved confidence in one's ability and judgments is achievement (Peplau, 1990). Consequently, it is difficult to understand how a client's self-concept could improve if a nurse is not committed to them and is not open to the client's experiences.

La Monica et al. (1987) explored the effect of nurses' empathy on the anxiety, depression, hostility and satisfaction with care of clients with cancer. They found less anxiety, depression and hostility in clients being cared for by nurses exhibiting high empathy.

La Monica's (1987) findings are further examples of the positive effect of emotional support. However, the outcomes reported in that study, and the others reported in this section, are dependent on the ability of nurses to offer high levels of empathy.

Bennett (1995) points out that research to date has only provided minimal evidence to support the view that clinical empathy in nursing affects health care outcomes. Nevertheless the cumulative research evidence across all helping professions indicates that the hypothesised relationship between empathy and helpful nurse-client relationships, remains a reasonable proposition. Additionally the evidence presented in Chapter 1 and this section indicates that unless nurses are able to offer a high level of empathy, they will be unable to understand the meaning of the client's experience. This assumption is supported also by the Mackay et al. (1990) finding that the quality of client self-disclosures was found to be associated with the level of empathy used by nurses.

2.2.3   The reported low levels of empathy in nursing

A considerable body of research exists to support the view that an interpersonal skill deficit exists in nursing practice. These reports are found mainly in the American and British literature, and relate to empathy.

Gow (1982) reported on an American study into how nurses' emotions in medical/surgical areas affect client care. Gow reported that about 60% of the nurses sampled (n = 550) were unable to look beyond an initial negative impression of the client. Duff and Hollingwood (1968) and La Monica et al. (1976) found that the majority of registered nurses tested showed extremely low levels of empathy. Gow suggested that willingness or unwillingness to look beyond clients' negative behaviour is a key factor in the balance between helpful relationships and unhelpful relationships.

Kershmer and La Monica (1976) investigated the level of empathy with undergraduate students immediately prior to and following their formal psychiatric nursing experience. The results indicated that all students scored a low level of empathy and that the facilitative conditions of relationship building were not acquired. These data were similar to the outcome of Reynolds' (1986) study with psychiatric nursing students in Scotland. Reynolds concluded, as did Kershmer and La Monica (1976), that a great deal of nurse education was ineffective in providing experiences necessary to prepare nurses to build empathic relationships.

These studies may explain why Towell (1975), Cormack (1975) and Reynolds (1982) found that psychiatric nurses in the United Kingdom were not making use of potentially therapeutic relationships in the manner that was described in much of the contemporary nursing literature. These researchers reported that nurses often found it difficult to respond to clients' direct requests for information, to discuss feelings with them, or to help clients focus on areas of concern.

Similarly, Melia (1981) reported that student nurses in medical/surgical areas often found it difficult to talk to clients about their illness, treatment, or personal problems. Compatible with these data is the outcome from a study conducted by McLeod-Clarke (1983) who found that nurse-client verbal interactions on surgical wards were generally of short duration, infrequent, and limited in content to physical and technical matters.

The McLeod-Clarke (1983) study may help explain the outcome from a follow-up study of women undergoing mastectomy for breast cancer which was conducted by Maguire (1985). During the study nurses were able to recognise only 20% of those women who had developed an anxiety state, depressive state, or body-image problem.

The McLeod-Clarke (1983) finding was replicated by Hughes and Carver (1990) who reported that a great deal of nurses' conversation related to aspects of treatment and caring. These researchers concluded that these interactions provided a clear demonstration of how nurses can manipulate conversations, possibly unconsciously to suit their own needs. Many nurses in this study were observed to enforce their wishes by simply not addressing specific concerns of clients. That is, the nurse did not show understanding of the client through verbal recognition of both client and affective dimensions of the client's message.

What should be of concern to nurse educators is that these studies and many others (e.g. Peitchinis, 1972; Layton, 1979; Wheeler and Barratt, 1994) identify common deficiencies in communication skills which relate to empathy and which are relevant to the stated objectives of nursing. A major objective of nursing relates to assessment of clients. It is important because it answers the question: "What is it that nurses ameliorate, change or prevent during clinical practice?" Unless nurse educators can discover and reduce the factors that cause the low levels of empathy in nursing, this objective is likely to remain difficult to attain. Failure to assess accurately the client's need for nursing is likely to result in care that does not meet the client's goals or allow the client to have an active part in problem-solving.

2.2.4 Potential consequences of low empathy nursing for clients

A concern about low empathy in nursing is that some clients who need to be understood by their nurse may not feel understood. Emotional withdrawal not only acts as a barrier to empathy, it interferes with the assessment phase of the nursing process. On occasions this might result in unfavourable health outcomes for these clients. This is suggested by numerous reports in the literature of clients who are at risk emotionally.

Tait (1985) stated that women who have developed breast cancer experience a special and unusually severe form of stress. Several studies suggest that women were more likely to experience depressive breakdown following a severe life event, such as mastectomy, if they lacked the opportunity to confide regularly in someone who understood them - a 'confiding tie' (Brown and Harris, 1978; Northouse, 1981; Denton and Baum, 1982; Bloom, 1982; McGuire and Van Dam, 1983).

An alternative group who may be at risk emotionally are the terminally ill. Freihofer and Felton (1976) identified nursing behaviours perceived to be most helpful to 25 fatally ill clients and their significant others. They reported that communication with the nurse, and her physical presence, was very highly valued. Communication described as helpful included an empathised awareness of the client's need to talk about death and dying.

These studies suggest that clients often experience health needs that have their origins in the original medical problem. These health needs are frequently psychosocial in nature, but they are not part of the disease diagnosed and treated by doctors. Concerns about body image, sexuality or death are human responses to actual and potential health problems that arise in day-to-day nurse-client relationships and which call for responsible, helpful nursing actions.

Such actions may include asking questions as, "What do you understand about your illness?" and, "What goes on when you feel misunderstood, worried, or lonely?" While Faulkner (1985) points out the importance of clients only receiving information for which they are ready, recognition of readiness is dependent upon an empathised awareness on the client's state of readiness. It is difficult to understand how this might happen unless nurses are encouraged to explore what the client wants to happen during verbal interactions (Larson, 1993).

The nursing literature suggests that there are many other reasons why nurses should be able to provide an empathised awareness of the client's experience. In relationship to breast cancer victims, several studies stress the importance of nurses meeting the information requirements regarding chemotherapy (Maetzinger and Dauber, 1982) and breast reconstruction (Rytledge, 1982). Much evidence exists to support the view that such information is beneficial to the client's post-operative progress (McLeod-Clarke, 1995). Finally, some writers (e.g. Ashworth, 1980; Tait, 1985; Marshfield, 1985; 1989) argue that clients who experience negative mood prior to, during, and following loss and change situations, need skilled counselling from nurses. Loss and change represent traumatic life events which frequently occur in acute medical/surgical units. Examples of loss and change include mutilating surgery, shortness of breath, and immobility. This suggests that there is a need for nurses to anticipate the information needs of their clients and to understand the meaning of the experience of the client. Failure to do so may mean that clients perceive the health-care system to be impersonal. Empathy provides a 'high touch' skill in health care environments in which health professionals need to use empathy to humanise care.

In psychiatric nursing contexts, nurses need to gain understanding of complex behaviours such as withdrawal, anxiety and dysfunctional family systems (Wilson and Kneisl, 1983; Raudonis, 1993). They need to understand the purpose of dysfunctional behaviour and what prevents people from giving up patterns of behaviour that reduce satisfaction with living. Nurses who work in psychiatric areas have opportunities to initiate relationships with clients, use them to help move the client in a direction favouring productive social living, and to learn about the purpose of dysfunctional behaviour (Peplau, 1988). The focus should be on the experience of the client, an outcome that is dependent on empathy. Otherwise the client's behaviour will not be understood and the nurse-client relationship may not contribute to restoration of health. It may even help to maintain illness patterns (Peplau, 1990; Smoyak, 1990).

Like all other helping professions, nursing ought to exist in order to help other people. The literature reviewed in the second section of this chapter (2.2) indicates that empathy is crucial to that fundamental aim and to a variety of nursing goals. It has been shown that:

a)   empathy enables nurses to create a climate of trust and to establish their clients' perception of need;

b)   it enables nurses to judge the client's state of readiness to talk;

c)   it is needed in order that nurses can understand the origins and purpose of clients' responses to health problems;

d)   several studies provide preliminary evidence that high-empathy nursing is likely to facilitate positive health outcomes for clients;

e)   positive health outcomes include reduction in physiological distress, improved self-concept and reduction in anxiety and depression;

f)   the achievement of such outcomes is dependent on the ability of nurses to offer high levels of empathy to their clients.

2.3 Summary of the absence of empathy

The literature reveals that like many other helping professionals, nurses do not generally offer much empathy to their clients. It has been shown that:

a)   low-empathy nursing is likely to mean that clients who need to be understood, may not be understood, or feel understood;

b)   failure to understand the needs of clients may mean that nurses fail to provide essential information, fail to provide emotional support, and in some instances may contribute to unfavourable health outcomes, such as increased distress, for those that they ought to be helping.

Due to the low level of empathy reported in nursing, there is a need for nurse educators to understand the cause of this problem. Explanations for the low level of clinical empathy in nursing are reviewed in Chapter 3.

3 Analysis: Empathy has not been measured in clients' terms and accordingly taught

In this chapter the remaining observations that motivated this study are examined. The first part focuses on the failure of measures of empathy to reflect clients' views, rather than professionals' views, about an ability to offer empathy. The second part examines the inconclusive research evidence that existing courses have enabled professionals to offer empathy, and the disagreement about how empathy is best taught. The literature reviewed in this chapter substantiates these observations.

3.1 The failure of existing measures of empathy to measure empathy in clients' terms

In this section it will be shown that:

a)   there is a need for an empathy scale that measures the concept of empathy in clients' terms;

b)   the client's perception of the helping relationship is not reflected in existing measures of empathy.

The importance of the client's perception of the helping process was emphasised within Egan's (1986) description of empathy. He suggested:

> it's the helper's way of saying I'm with you, I've been listening carefully to what you've been saying and expressing, and I'm checking if my understanding is accurate (p 99).

If clients are able to perceive the amount and nature of empathy existing in a helping relationship, they are in a position to advise professionals about how to offer empathy. Such a collaborative process would enable the client's view about helpful behaviour to be reflected in scales developed to measure the degree of empathy existing in a helping relationship. This need is indicated by Rogers (1975) and Gladstein's (1977) claim that clients are better judges of the degree of empathy than therapists.

In spite of Rogers' (1975) suggestion that clients know a considerable amount about how to offer empathy, this appears to have been ignored in the construction of existing measures of empathy. The failure to measure empathy in clients' terms is suggested by the manner in which scale items were selected for the most commonly used measures of cognitive-behavioural empathy.

Carkhuff and Truax (1967) inform us that the items on the Accurate Empathy Scale originated from a seminar with Rogers in 1957. Later, advice and comments were received from colleagues and psychology students. Carkhuff and Truax conceded that the scale, which represented professional views of empathy, was a crude attempt to specify the meaning of the construct.

Statements making up the Barrett-Lennard Relationship Inventory were derived from Rogers' (1957) paper on client-centered therapy. Experts from the University of Chicago Counselling Centre were invited to comment on and revise the initial scale items. This approach established the extent to which the scale items represented all behaviours that the instrument intended to measure.

The development of the Empathy Construct Rating scale (La Monica, 1981) involved the collection of statements from fifty graduate students (nursing and psychology) which described a person who exhibited either well developed empathy and lack of empathy. These statements were reviewed by the investigator and two research assistants. Two hundred and fifteen items were selected from an initial item pool of 500 statements, 90 of which were negative and 125 were positive. Finally, the remaining statements were rated by a panel of experts, university professors in the fields of psychometrics, clinical psychology and nursing. The items rated by any of the experts as unclear indicators were deleted.

While it is not being suggested that the views of professionals are unimportant, the construction of existing measures of empathy seems somewhat one-sided. The approach adopted is analogous to educators identifying effective characteristics of a supervisory relationship, without identifying the views of students. In such circumstances it is difficult to be certain that all items on an empathy scale measure behaviour that is perceived by clients to be helpful. In addition clients may have perceptions that contribute to our understanding of empathic relationships.

In this section, it has been argued that clients' perceptions of helping relationships would inform nurse educators about empathy skills needed by nurses. In order to assess nurses' ability to display empathy there is a need for a measure of empathy that reflects what clients feel that nurses ought to be doing within the nurse-client relationship. This is indicated by the suggestions in the literature (Rogers, 1975; Gladstein, 1977; Egan, 1986) that clients are a rich source of information about the application of empathy in helping relationships. The development of an instrument that measures empathy in clients' terms is likely to clarify the construct of empathy within nursing practice. Consequently, it is suggested here that there is a need to develop a valid measure of nurses' ability to offer empathy, in clients' terms, that measures that ability reliably. The lack of such an instrument is one limitation of existing empathy courses.

3.2 Limitations of existing empathy courses

In this section, it will be shown that:

a)   there is uncertainty about what is being taught and learned
         on existing empathy courses;
b)   there is confusion about which components of empathy
         education are effective;
c)   there is disagreement about what is meant by experiential
         learning and whether classroom learning can be replicated in
         clinical areas.

3.2.1 The confusion about what is being taught and learned

Several attempts to teach empathy have been reported in the literature. However, it is often unclear what is being taught on many of those programmes and whether what is being taught reflects clients' views of empathy. While some of those teaching programmes have been described as interpersonal skill training, rather than empathy training, they are mentioned because the authors (Dietrich, 1978; Briggs, 1982; Marson, 1982; Anderson, 1984) have implied that their teaching programmes were relevant to the teaching and learning of empathy.

Major limitations of those programmes were the failure to define empathy operationally and to describe the interpersonal theory on which the training programme was based. This made assessment difficult. Therefore, there is confusion about what to teach and learn because assessment often informs the learning process (Gronlund, 1981). Teaching programmes described as interpersonal skill training have tended to focus on interpersonal techniques which may contribute to empathy rather than the theory which underpins this approach to helping. For example, Anderson's (1994) teaching programme concentrated on the techniques of i) reflecting the client's feelings, ii) reflecting the content of the client's communication, and iii) avoidance of leading or directing the client.

The extent to which a training programme which emphasises a pre-selected range of techniques or skills can be successful is open to speculation. Reynolds (1994) has noted that unless students have available an extensive repertoire of responding strategies, they can experience difficulty in coping with the varying degrees of clinical problems presented by clients. Such problems include the client's ability, or willingness, to make self-disclosures.

3.2.1.1 The variability of approaches to assessment A problem is that empathy courses have assessed different things. Consequently it is not known what they actually teach and it is difficult to say how effective they are. The variation in assessment methods has made the comparison of success across training programmes difficult. Detterman and Sternberg (1982) propose that a common set of criteria for evaluating skills-orientated programmes would be useful in achieving some basic uniformity of standards of teaching and assessment.

Some writers have failed to report how their learning outcomes were assessed (Dietrich, 1978; Marson, 1979). While these writers claimed that experiential learning methods enabled nurses to improve the quality of interpersonal communications, no evidence was provided to support this assertion.

Assessment of learning during several teaching programmes has tended to consist of unstructured data obtained from students' diaries, or from formal and informal discussions with students (e.g. Thompson et al. 1965; Briggs, 1982; Zoske and Pietrocarlo, 1983). This approach to assessment relies upon students' subjective impressions of learning. While it is possible that learning occurred as a consequence of these teaching programmes, the extent to which learning outcomes related to the aims of teaching programmes or whether self-perception reflected students' ability to offer empathy in real clinical situations is unclear.

By contrast, several studies which examined an approach to teaching empathy utilised existing measures of the construct. These instruments and studies include the Accurate Empathy Scale (Carkhuff and Truax, 1965; Kalish, 1971), the empathy subscale of the Barrett-Lennard Relationship Inventory (Law, 1978; Kirk, 1979; Layton, 1979), the Hogan Empathy Scale (Brockhaus et al, 1971) and the Empathy Construct Rating Scale (La Monica, 1983). These instruments, with the exception of the Hogan Empathy Scale (a measure of moral empathy), are measures of cognitive-behavioural empathy and represent the most frequently used measures for empathy research at the present time (see McKay et al., 1990; Layton et al., 1990).

A challenge facing investigators wanting to investigate learning outcomes of empathy training is to identify those specific behaviours which indicate empathy. Differing approaches toward the operationalisation of empathy make this a difficult task.

Further examination of the literature reveals that operational definitions of empathy proposed by researchers and teachers are not always conceptually compatible with the measuring instrument selected. For example, Brockhaus et al. (1971) defined empathy in cognitive-behavioural terms and then selected the Hogan Empathy Scale, a measure of trait/moral empathy, to evaluate learning outcomes of their training programme.

The Hogan Empathy Scale is a 64-item, self-reporting measure and is not specifically orientated to a counselling context. The choice of this instrument seems odd given that programme aims included developing skill in understanding and communicating therapeutically. Perhaps unsurprisingly, the experimental programme did not result in significant change among subjects' scores on the Hogan Scale.

During a follow-up study the investigators chose a different outcome criterion. Clinical interviews were taped and rated by using Carkhuff's Empathic Understanding Scale. This outcome measure seemed more compatible with the investigators' aim of developing in psychiatric aides the ability to be more empathic when interacting with clients.

Even when the operational definition of empathy seems compatible with the measuring instrument, the extent to which the stated learning outcomes of training are reflected adequately by items on the instrument needs to be considered. Teachers have tended to develop course objectives and then select an existing measure of empathy. While it is arguable that learning outcomes can be assessed by scores on an instrument, this tendency may be problematic for two reasons.

Firstly, because empathy instruments have evolved from different professional contexts, the question needs to be asked, "To what extent does an instrument developed to measure counselling or psychotherapy, replicate empathy in traditional nurse-client relationships?" The issue alluded to here relates to practical utility across professions.

Secondly, the reliability of the most commonly used empathy scales is unclear. The reliability of the Truax Accurate Empathy Scale, and the Barrett-Lennard Relationship Inventory, have been questioned by some writers (e.g. Bachrach, 1976 and Gagan, 1983). This raises the possibility that it may not always be clear what is being measured by those scales.

Fielding et al. (1987) and Coates and Chambers (1992) suggest that in the area of evaluating nurses' communication skills, too often the need to assess is sacrificed to the goal of getting something done. Alternatively, the literature cited in this section suggests that inappropriate means of assessment may sometimes be selected.

If assessment of learning provides accurate information about the individual nurse's thoughts and actions in particular nursing situations, training is more likely to be effective (Gronlund, 1981). In addition to its role in the planning of training, assessment provides the baseline for the later evaluation of change and the effectiveness of training.

Due to the methodological concerns cited in section 3.1 an empathy scale was developed for this study which enabled the investigator to ask questions about learning outcomes which related to course aims. The course, which will be described later, was designed to teach nurses to offer empathy in clients' terms.

3.2.2 *The confusion about which components of empathy education are effective*

Issues relevant to empathy education are how and where it is best taught and learned. Several classroom methods of teaching interpersonal skills and/or empathy have been described in the literature. Teaching programmes have differed in terms of teaching methods, length of programmes, and the extent to which learning is focused in the classroom, or during clinical practice. This suggests a lack of agreement among educators about which components of education and training empower students to learn how to offer empathy to clients.

3.2.2.1 Learning in the classroom Generally, classroom methods of teaching empathy have been described as experiential learning in small groups. Numerous writers (eg. Dietrich, 1976; Thompson et al., 1965; Kalish, 1971; Layton, 1979; Marsen, 1979; Zoske et al., 1983; La Monica, 1983; Allcock, 1992; Dowie and Park, 1988) have suggested that experiential learning is an effective way of teaching and learning empathy skills.

Experiential learning methods evolved from the theorising of Dewey (1958) who argued that all educational processes should be based on the life experiences of students and that school experiences and life experiences should be directly linked in a planned programme. It has been suggested by contributors to the nursing literature (eg. Waterworth, 1995; Burnard, 1995) that three key elements go to make up the concept of experiential learning. These are:

a) personal experience;
b) reflection on experience;
c) the transformation of thinking and behaviour.

However, the concept has been used to describe a variety of educational approaches that vary in their focus and intent.

Burnard (1992a) described the disagreement that appears to exist in this area. He examined nurse teachers' perceptions of experiential learning and reported that they found it difficult to define the concept. Burnard reported that they had less difficulty in citing examples of what they would call experiential learning. Examples could be divided into two groups: (i) experiential learning in clinical areas, and (ii) activities which teachers use in classrooms. The respondents talked more of the second category than the first. Examination of Burnard's data revealed that teachers tended to view experiential learning as learning from and involving a student-centred focus. However, disagreement existed among teachers about whether experiential learning involved reflection on experience in the past, or in the present time.

The problem indicated by this finding is that many nurse educators are uncertain about what experiential learning means. In such circumstances it is difficult to be confidant that they know how to provide types of experiential situations that will help nurses to learn how to offer empathy.

Later, Burnard (1992b) reported that student nurses viewed experiential learning differently from teachers. While teachers tended to view the concept as a series of classroom activities, students tended to describe it as seeing and doing in the 'here and now' of the clinical world. Additionally, some students considered experiential activities such as role play in the classroom to be artificial. This is a point which merits teachers' consideration and wider exploration.

The views expressed by nurses in Burnard's (1992b) research reveal that they expressed a preference for experiential learning that matched the reality of clinical practice. This requires that nurse educators set up situations that allow a student to gain new insight and skills through participation with clients. Several writers (e.g. McGinnis, 1987; Farkas-Cameron, 1995; Malby, 1997) suggest that such an experiential process can be effective if nurses are provided with an experienced and trusted adviser (a mentor) who can assist them to think and question themselves. However, nurse educators have tended to use experiential workshops as a method of teaching empathy skills. The diversity of experiential methods used suggests a lack of common agreement about what works best, and where learning should occur. The following empathy courses for nurses illustrate this problem.

Kalish (1971) reported that her empathy programme involved the integration of four elements i) didactic training, ii) some experiential training in communication skills, iii) role playing, and iv) a role model of empathy. In this case, experiential learning did not involve role play or role modelling. According to Kalish, the experiential component consisted of viewing films and tapes of therapeutic interviews. Students were then asked to respond in writing and then verbally, to the client as if they were the actual helper. In contrast, Farrel et al. (1977) used only two of these approaches: role playing exercises, and the viewing of videotape vignettes of counselling interviews.

Kalish (1971) suggested that viewing films and tapes of therapeutic interviews is experiential learning. The extent to which this method promotes examination of personal experience is open to speculation. Confusion about experiential learning is suggested also by Farrel et al. (1977) assumption that role play is experiential learning, a view not shared by Kalish. Furthermore, the fact that Kalish and Farrel et al. used different course components emphasises a lack of agreement about what it is that facilitates an empathic nurse. This confusion is highlighted further by the following studies of empathy education.

La Monica (1993 and 1987) reported that she used six teaching modes - didactic techniques, experiential techniques, modelling, rehearsal, feedback and imagery. In this case experiential learning was defined as encouraging individuals to examine their experiences in depth. La Monica described imagery as being reflection on the personal vicarious experiences of another person, a process that seems somewhat synonymous with examining experiences in depth.

Of interest is the question: "Which learning experiences were effective in empowering students to display high levels of empathy?" The central importance of this question is indicated by a study conducted by Hughes et al. (1990). Those researchers described their empathy training programme as experiential learning in small groups, consisting of modelling and feedback. Like La Monica (1983), these writers claimed that their training programme was effective but failed to identify effective course components. The question raised here relates directly to the second research question probed by this study. The question was: Which components of empathy education affect nurses' ability to offer empathy?

In view of the barriers to the utilisation of interpersonal skills in nursing cited in Chapter 2, experiential learning in the classroom could be considered to be a pragmatic solution to the problem of low empathy nursing. Numerous contributors to the nursing literature imply that it is possible to learn skills by reflecting retrospectively on past experience in a classroom. This view is often defended by citing the thinking of theorists who have proposed that reflection on experience can result in more effective behaviour (e.g. Boydell, 1976; Kolb, 1984; Schon, 1987; Burnard and Chapman, 1990). The general view expressed by these writers is that learning involves the student working out things by restructuring their perceptions of what is happening. However, the extent to which skills acquired can be applied to a clinical work environment seems unresolved (McGinnis, 1987).

3.2.2.2 Learning in clinical contexts Alternative views about the context of teaching can be found in the literature. Nicol and Withington (1981), Ellis and Watson (1985) and Costello (1989) argued that practical rooms within the school of nursing are of little value in teaching practical nursing skills as it is more appropriate to learn these skills in clinical areas. In this vein, Alexander (1983) and Smith (1995) observed that the clinical area is the most fertile area for learning. As Peplau (1957) suggested, what students actually experience when clients express feelings such as anxiety, worthlessness, or anger, influences these situations. This suggests that reflection on clinical experience in the 'here and now' might be an effective form of experiential learning because it involves the emotional aspect of the individual's experience. In support of this view, Murphy (1971) suggested that the student's perception of her effectiveness during clinical work and the client's expressed reaction offer the most valid evaluation of the effectiveness of the curriculum in the preparation of practitioners. This view from the American literature was echoed in the British literature by Bendall (1976) who stated that "...we must regain our perception that the central core of nurse training and education lies in the reality of clinical patient care" (p 7).

Clinton (1985), while recognising that research into nurse education has stressed that the clinical learning environment is the main influence on what and how students learn argued that equal attention should be given to nurses' classroom education. In keeping with this view, some educators have incorporated a combination of classroom and clinical teaching within their empathy training programmes. Both elements involved a number of experiential, student-centered activities. Three studies emphasise how classroom teaching and clinical work with clients can be merged.

A study conducted by Carkhuff and Truax (1965) involved asking trainees to rate therapist ability during taped samples of counselling, and then to formulate responses to taped client statements. Following this workshop experience their initial clinical interview with a real client was recorded and rated on the Truax Accurate Empathy Scale. What is not known is whether classroom work, clinical work, or the combination of both resulted in improved scores on the AES.

Lewis (1974) employed a similar approach to the Carkhuff and Truax Study (1965). Different elements included the use of simulated clients (actors) as well as real clients, and the employment of different rating scales. The Carkhuff Empathic Understanding Scale and a nine point global measure of empathy were utilised during training. Why simulated and real clients were used was not explained. There was a lack of analysis of the most effective course components.

Juneck et al. (1979) employed a method of teaching empathy that involved teaching in a group setting. During this teaching programme supervisors, students and a client were present in the same room. Clinical work consisted of supervisors and students demonstrating empathy toward the client. Following this, clients were invited to comment on their thoughts and feelings during the clinical interview and to provide any feedback for the interviewer that they were able to give. Once the client left, the student gave a critique of the interview and received advice from the supervisor. The effective components of this course are unknown.

While these teaching programmes did include course work that matched the reality of clinical practice, the most effective course components remain unclear. Since the literature does not specify in adequate detail which components of empathy education are effective, it is important to learn what exactly helps nurses to learn how to offer empathy. There would seem to be a need, therefore, to investigate further how high empathy nursing is best achieved. It is important to understand how nurses learn about empathy by investigating what they think about their learning experiences, and the consequences for them, as learners and clinicians.

3.2.3 Summary of limitations of existing empathy courses

In this section, it has been shown that:

a) there is confusion about what is being taught on many courses due to the failure to define empathy operationally;
b) the variation in assessment methods has made the outcomes of different training programmes difficult to compare;

c) there is confusion about what is being learned on existing courses because assessment is sometimes based on perception of participants (teachers and students), and doubts exist about the reliability, validity and practical utility of existing measures of empathy;

d) there is lack of analysis of the components of empathy education which affect helpers' ability to offer empathy in clinical contexts;

e) concerns about whether existing courses can enable nurses to learn how to offer empathy to actual clients, indicate that there remains a need to develop an effective way of teaching nurses to show empathy.

The research evidence that existing courses can help nurses to learn how to show empathy is inconclusive. The studies cited in the next section indicate that there is a need to investigate further how high empathy nursing is best achieved.

3.3   Evidence that existing courses do not help nurses to learn to show empathy

The outcomes from studies of empathy education do not encourage the view that existing courses could help nurses to show high levels of empathy. The questions raised by these studies suggest that it is unlikely that any of the existing courses could improve the low level of empathy in clinical nursing, or that we know best how to do this.

While most studies of empathy training programmes encourage the view that empathy can be learned, the conclusions based on existing research require further investigation. The results of those studies are inconclusive due to conflicting results, issues relating to study design, the extent to which training gains were maintained and what exactly, accounted for those gains. Studies varied as to the amount of time in the training process, varying from 5-12 hours (Kalish, 1971), to 100 hours (Carkhuff and Truax, 1965). This suggests that the optimum length of empathy training has still to be settled.

3.3.1 The limitations of study designs

Many studies of empathy training have been methodologically weak. Most studies have relied upon a non-experimental design. The failure to control other variables that might have affected the outcome makes it difficult to be confident about the hypothesised relationship between training and learning. Additionally, all studies have raised questions that merit further exploration and more detailed explication. The questions are illustrated by the studies reported in this section.

Lewis (1974) described a course designed to give trainee psychotherapists an opportunity to have practical experience of empathic ways of responding to the affective elements of a client's communication. In spite of the training emphasis upon an interaction with simulated clients and clinical work with real clients, the Hogan Empathy Scale, a measure of trait empathy, was used in order to have a base point from which to evaluate change in the subjects' empathy. A major concern is that the assessment instrument was not compatible with the aims of the course.

Junek et al. (1978) study demonstrated an improvement in empathy for first year psychiatric residents following a series of seminars in interviewing skills. The focus for this programme was the direction of students towards the process of interviewing as opposed to the content of the interview. Segments of videotaped interviews of residents taken before and after training were rated blindly by trained raters on a modified version of the Barrett Lennard Relationship Inventory. Data from raters were subjected to analysis of variance (ANOVA). Significant difference was found among measures (p>.001).

Junek et al. acknowledged that the lack of a control group make it difficult to be certain about variables that may have caused the result. Additionally, the small number of subjects who completed the course (n =5) makes it difficult to be certain about the extent to which the method and results are generalisable. Caution is indicated by the failure of one resident to complete his videotaped interviews because he felt too insecure to expose himself on videotape. Hung and Rosenthal (1978) point out that videotaping can produce self-consciousness and anxiety. The playback must be handled sensitively and with care. This suggests that the use of videotape might not be suitable for all subjects.

La Monica et al. (1976) reported that while intensive empathy training significantly raised nurses' levels of empathy, more training was needed to enable all subjects to help another person successfully. This poses the question: "How much time is necessary to develop the empathic nurse?" Additionally, one might wonder whether there are individuals who would be unlikely to benefit from empathy training. This question seems important in view of Layton's (1979) suggestion that empathy may be relatively stable and resistant to change in some subjects. Alternatively, it could be asked: "What type of education is needed to help these subjects to learn how to offer empathy?"

Hughes et al. (1990) reported that the effectiveness of their empathy training programme for nurses was evaluated in terms of changes in rating of empathy calculated before and after training. An adaptation of the Carkhuff Empathetic Understanding Scale (modified by Gazda et al. 1975) was used as a measure of empathy. Measurements were made by judges using pre and post-tests of learner-client interaction, in a laboratory setting.

The post-training ratings showed increased ability to use empathy with a simulated client. The mean rating on the written post-test was 2.975 and on the spoken test was 2.875 (p<.005). Because all subjects (n = 11) gained increased scores among measures, Hughes et al. (1990) concluded that the outcome had clinical significance. However, the assumption that learners can transfer laboratory learning to clinical practice with real clients remains a hypothesis which requires testing.

Whether ratings based on responses to selected client statements yield accurate estimates of helpers' empathy needs to be investigated. Arguably responses to a client's often confused messages need to be based upon the entire flow and context of the client's narrative, rather than an isolated segment of communication.

3.3.2 Experimental study designs

Some studies have attempted to improve research methodology by using control groups to make comparisons with the experimental group. Results from these studies have been promising but inconclusive.

A study conducted by Carkhuff and Truax (1965) involved the supervisors didactically teaching the student the former's accumulated clinical and research knowledge concerning effective therapeutic behaviours which facilitate empathy. Experiential learning was then provided which required students to rate therapist ability during taped samples of counselling. Further, students were invited to formulate responses to taped client statements. In addition students role-played and finally, their initial clinical interviews with clients were recorded and rated. The Truax Accurate Empathy Scale was utilised for all evaluations of empathy. It was found that in respect of empathy, the students could be brought to function at levels of effective therapy quite similar to those of more experienced counsellors in less than 100 hours of training.

While that study is encouraging, Rappaport and Chinsky (1972) expressed doubt about the reliability and validity of the Accurate Empathy Scale as a measure of empathy. This raises doubts about whether the AES measures empathy. Also, the course did not involve nurses. This raises doubt about whether the aims of the course are relevant to nursing contexts. Finally, the long-term effects of that training programme have not been established.

3.3.3 Concern about clinical significance

A concern about existing empathy education is whether the outcomes have value for the realities of clinical practice. The purpose of Brockhaus et al. (1971) study was to train 10 psychiatric aides in an experimental group to respond at level 3 on Carkhuff's Accurate Empathic Understanding Scale. At this level accurate exploration of deep feelings is initiated by the helper. The training programme included role play, group discussion, and training tapes. No supervised clinical practice was provided. The outcome criteria were taped interviews with trained clients pre-course, post-course, and delayed post-course, on the AES. This study indicated that both control and experimental groups increased in empathic level. The experimental group showed the largest gain. Delayed post-course data revealed that this gain was maintained at least 6 weeks after termination of training.

However, even though the changes in the experimental group were statistically significant (p<.05), the mean levels for the group did not reach the minimum therapeutic level of 3.0 on the AES. Brockhaus et al. suggested that the 6 weeks of training needed to be extended to 11 weeks in order to enable subjects to reach the minimum therapeutic level. This view was based on an assumption that the base rate of change could be maintained when extending the training programme.

Of further interest is the extent to which practice with clients trained to volunteer a personal feeling replicates actual clinical work. Studies of clients' perceptions of the helping relationship suggest otherwise. Clients have reported for example, that they are often unable or unwilling to express themselves when the helper is perceived to be threatening (e.g. Dittes, 1957; Reynolds, 1986). This suggests the need to be cautious in generalising from studies which purportedly are investigating a general class of phenomena but which in actuality are studying a limited fragment of the phenomena in question. For this reason, Brockhaus et al. (1971) experimental study, and many others (e.g. Kalish, 1971; Farrell et al., 1977) seem quite artificial, particularly as a very limited amount of time is used to study the phenomena under investigation.

If research studies are to have value for the realities of the training situation, then they must bear some definite resemblance to those situations (Dawson et al., 1984; McKay et al., 1990). Experiential training, for example, may include a wide variety of activities, some of which may be of more direct value than others. Teachers and researchers need to be more specific in delineating what they believe are critical aspects of such training, define them operationally, and then study them in situations which bear some correspondence to the actual training situations. At the present time, the findings secured from experimental studies, conducted in laboratories, are frequently inconclusive and occasionally contradictory.

3.4 Summary of the reasons for absence of empathy

In this chapter, it has been shown that existing measures of empathy do not reflect adequately clients' views about the ability to offer empathy. It has been suggested that clients' perceptions of the helping relationship enables them to advise nurses and other helping professionals about the degree of empathy existing in a relationship. This advice is likely to clarify the meaning of the construct of empathy in clinical nursing and define the aims of empathy courses for nurses.

The need for new ways of helping nurses to offer clinical empathy is indicated by the low levels of empathy in nursing and the limitations of existing empathy courses. These courses do not clearly help nurses or other professionals to offer empathy, particularly in clinical contexts. The literature reveals that:

a)   we do not know what the optimum length of an empathy course should be;

b)   there is no common agreement about which components of an empathy course are effective;

c) we do not know clearly whether existing measures of an ability to offer empathy are reliable and valid;

d) we do not know clearly what the long-term consequences of empathy training are for nurse-client relationships;

e) most studies of empathy education have been methodologically weak.

It has been concluded that empathy education needs to have relevance to the real training situation where it matters. Measures of outcome need to reflect what clients want from nurses and the aims of courses. While there is disagreement about where empathy is best learned, it is suggested that clinically focused education may be more meaningful to nurses because it provides them with information about their relationships with actual clients. Unless nurse educators can devise effective ways of resolving the low level of empathy in nursing, it is likely that their clients will perceive care as impersonal, that they will not receive necessary emotional support and may suffer long term consequences, such as reduced satisfaction with living.

4 Solution, Part 1: A reliable and valid client-centred empathy scale has now been developed

This chapter consists of four parts. First, the rationale for developing a reliable and valid client-centred measure of empathy is explained. Secondly, the development of a new client-centred empathy scale is described. Thirdly, the features of the new scale are discussed. Finally, the evaluation of the new measuring scale for reliability and validity, and the results of these investigations, are described.

4.1 Need: For a measure of empathy that enables nurses to know when they are showing empathy

In this section, it will be shown that:

a) there was a need for a measure of empathy that measures what nurses ought to be doing during their relationships with clients;
b) clients' perceptions of the helping relationship are a rich source of information about the application of empathy to clinical nursing;
c) there was a need to develop a measure of nurses' ability to offer empathy that yields consistent results among measures (reliability) and does measure what it is intended to measure (validity).

A major problem faced by nurses is knowing when they are showing empathy. Aspey (1975) identified that some professionals think that the helping relationship is a mystical process rather than a deliberate application of learned skills. Similarly, Reynolds (1986) reported that most nurse educators interviewed were unclear about how they defined and assessed empathy. This suggests that there is a need for an instrument that enables nurses, and others, to know when they are showing empathy.

While clinical nursing does involve one-to-one verbal interactions with clients, the literature review suggests that these do not necessarily replicate formal counselling or psychotherapy relationships. Some existing measures of empathy were not developed to measure empathy displayed within nurse-client relationships and so they are likely to be inappropriate measures of nurses ability to offer empathy. The Accurate Empathy Scale and the Barrett-Lennard Relationship Inventory were intended to be applied within the context of psychotherapy interactions, consequently they may have limited application to less formal nurse-client relationships.

By contrast, the Empathy Construct Rating Scale was developed by La Monica (1981) for use among nursing and other health professionals who are in positions of giving help, and who are in positions of authority relative to the recipients of care. The scale is concerned with initiating supportive interpersonal communication, and the focus of empathy is the other person who is in need of affective support. Items such as: "Does not have a ready answer to problems, but rather supported a person until she/he reaches a solution." and "Is tactless and curt." appear to be orientated to the nurse's working day, in other words, what nurses actually do during ongoing relationships with clients. Thus the scale appears to measure what Cormack (1985) refers to as the unique use of interpersonal skills in nursing. However, a major limitation of the scale is the lack of clear operational definitions of scale items, and doubts about the reliability of the instrument, which will be discussed later.

4.1.1 *The importance of clients' perceptions of the helping relationship*

Earlier, in Chapter 3, it was suggested that it is the client's perception of the helping relationship that determines whether the helper is empathic or not. For this reason it is arguable that clients' perceptions of their relationships with nurses can contribute to the clarification of the meaning of empathy within nursing practice. The way in which clients see nurses as being effective or ineffective listeners is likely to be a rich source of information about how they would like their relationships with nurses to be. Such insights would inform nurse educators about what clients want from nurses, help identify empathic skills needed by nurses, and provide a basis for the development of a measure of nurses' ability to offer empathy.

4.1.2 *The importance of a reliable and valid measure of empathic behaviour*

A concern for researchers is the extent to which measures of empathic skills are reliable and valid. A review of the literature reveals some doubt about whether existing measures of cognitive-behavioural empathy yield consistent results among measures (reliability) and do measure what they purport to measure (validity).

A concern about the Truax Accurate Empathy Scale is that reliability, derived from inter-rater comparisons, sometimes descend to unacceptable levels (Shapiro, 1969; Rogers, 1967). Marshall (1977) states that individual studies by Truax and Carkhuff (1967) frequently do not specify in adequate detail how ratings are actually made. Truax and Mitchell (1971) made it clear that the scale is used in a variable manner.

In view of the doubt expressed about the scale's reliability, caution must also be expressed about the scale's validity. Bachrach (1976) posed the question: *"What is being measured by the Accurate Empathy Scale?"* This writer expressed the view that it may be more difficult to make Accurate Empathy ratings than Truax implies. Bachrach (1974) had earlier suggested that ratings of empathic relationship qualities are strongly associated with evaluative dimensions in the rater's mind (for example, good/nice). Similarly Rappaport and Chinsky (1972) argued that the construct Accurate Empathy is markedly confused. Two studies, Caracena and Vicory (1969) and Truax (1976) lend evidence to the difficulty of understanding the meaning of the AES. These studies found empathy ratings to be significantly and positively related to the number of words spoken by the therapist. Caracena and Vicory interpreted their data as being congruent with the Kiesler, Mathieu and Klein (1967) hypothesis that something other than empathy was being measured.

In spite of the fairly high reliability estimates obtained with the Barrett-Lennard Relationship Inventory some caution may be necessary. Polit and Hungler (1983) point out that the reliability of an instrument is not the property of an instrument but rather of an instrument when administered to a certain sample under specific conditions. This suggests a possible instability in the instrument when applied to nursing studies, rather than psychotherapy interactions. Hospital nursing does not usually entail the commitment of one nurse to one client in an ongoing relationship, although widespread adoption of the nursing process and/or primary nursing may change this. Gagan (1983) suggests that there is a need for an empathy measure which is more specifically orientated towards the traditional nurse-client relationship. While Gagan's study did involve nurses talking to clients for prolonged periods, the extent to which that replicated formal psychotherapy was a concern.

While initial investigations of the Empathy Construct Rating Scale are encouraging, a note of caution is suggested by La Monica's (1987) report that empathy training failed to result in significant changes in client and self-reported empathy following that programme. La Monica conceded that the results of this study call into question the ability of the ECRS to discriminate among high levels of empathy when subjects (pre-test) are rated highly on the instrument. She suggests further that the social desirability of scale items may affect self-ratings and client ratings. If this were the case, the validity of the ECRS as a measure of the construct is called into question.

This possibility is suggested by Reynolds' (1986) study of student nurses' empathy. Reynolds reported that while change occurred among some measures (self-reports, charge nurse, client and trained raters) on the ECRS, those changes were generally small and/or non significant. Furthermore, there was a tendency for different methods of scoring the ECRS (self reports, client reports) not to correlate highly with each other. Reynolds suggested that it was possible that different criteria were applied among raters to make the ratings. This suggests a problem with reliability and poses the questions, "What was being measured by different respondents?" This raises doubt about the appropriateness of the instrument when the goal is to investigate the effectiveness of empathy training. It suggests also that there is a need to develop a new measure of nurses' ability to offer empathy, that reflects the views of clients, and to investigate that measure for reliability and validity.

4.2 Method: Development phases of a client-centred empathic-behavioural scale

In this section, it will be shown that:

a)   there was a need for a measure of empathy which measured the intended outcomes of the empathy course that is the focus of this study;

b)   an initial source of items on the new empathy scale was clients' reports of what was effective and ineffective about relationships with nurses;

c)   the development of the item pool into a Likert Scale provided an opportunity to obtain summated scores for the scale and a means of investigating the effectiveness of a new empathy course.

4.2.1 Overview of Development Phases

Three phases were used in the development of the empathy scale. Each phase is discussed in greater detail later in this section. Firstly the researcher reviewed his personal experience and published knowledge about the measurement of empathy. This was done in order to determine whether existing empathy scales could enable nurses to know when they are showing empathy.

Secondly clients' perceptions of effective and ineffective interpersonal behaviours were studied. This was done in order to construct an item pool for a client-centred measure of empathy. Clients' perceptions were compared with professionals' views of empathy. This was done in order to establish at an early stage whether clients' perceptions of helping were congruent with professionals' views.

Finally, the item pool was developed into a Likert Scale. This was done in order to rank nurses' performance on each item on the empathy scale. In order to guide scorers of the empathy scale a user's manual was developed. This was done in order to ensure that the scale was a reliable measure of empathy.

4.2.2 Phase 1: The recognition of the need for a measure of empathy that reflects clients' views

Clients' contributions towards understanding the nature of the empathic process are an important component of establishing the validity of any learning outcomes for empathy education. This reflects the growing consensus that the consumer of health care is an important, active collaborator in treatment and outcome goals (Barker, 1994; Highland Health Board, 1994; The Scottish Office, 1997). Since existing measures did not measure empathy in clients' terms, and due to concerns about the reliability and validity of existing measures of cognitive-behavioural empathy, it was recognised that it was necessary to develop a new measure of empathy a new measure of empathy that reflects clients' views. The items on the empathy scale that were subsequently developed reflect the intended outcomes of a new empathy course.

4.2.3 Phase 2: The source of items on the scale

An initial source of insight into clients' perceptions of the empathic process was unsolicited comments made by clients to the researcher during previous empathy research (Reynolds, 1986). These comments were made during client ratings (n=30) of basic student nurses on the Empathy Construct Rating Scale (La Monica, 1981), which followed supervised clinical practice. The statements, which were relatively unprompted, often consisted of expanded explanations for their assessment of nurses' empathy on the scale being used at that time. These anecdotal statements were of interest because they described clients' reasons for perceiving a nurse to be effective or ineffective in terms of building a type of relationship that Rogers (1975) terms empathic. The statements were noted and retained for future analysis by the researcher and teaching colleagues.

While it is possible to argue that clients might view nurses as being highly empathic, whether they are or not, the richness of these data suggests that clients were describing their actual experiences with nurses. These descriptions included the extent to which they experienced sensitive understanding and freedom from defensiveness, suggesting validity of the data. This argument is supported by Oppenheim's (1992) suggestion that validity with qualitative data can be established by the openness and depth of information being obtained.

In spite of the limitations that may apply to the perceptions of clients, some contributors to the research literature have defended this method of studying a complex phenomenon. An example is Cormack (1981) who expressed the view that unsolicited and spontaneous comments may add to our understanding of the general area being researched. Rogers (1975) and Gladstein (1977) go further, claiming that clients are better judges of the degree of empathy than therapists. Rogers (1975) seems to have little or no objection to prompting clients, and suggests that...

> perhaps if we wish to become better therapists, we should let our clients tell us whether we are understanding them accurately (p 6).

An examination of clients' descriptions of their experiences with nurses in Reynolds' (1986) study supported Rogers' and Gladstein's assumptions that clients know a great deal about the degree of empathy existing in a relationship. These data suggest that their experience of the nurse-client relationship is a fertile source of information about the phases of the empathic relationship, and about how it is best brought about. The conclusions drawn from these data were subsequently reinforced by a study of numerous audiotaped records of nurse-client relationships in various clinical settings (n=200) and several years of observing teacher-learner relationships. This further encouraged the view that the perceptions of the client group reported here may be generalised to other recipients of the helping relationship.

An examination of the clients' statements by the researcher and two colleagues resulted in the identification of four variables that are critical to the empathic relationship. At that time, the researcher's objective was to design and develop an empathy education programme that has some basis in clients' perceptions of the experience of being helped by professionals. It was recognised that these variables may not be the only ones important to the helping relationship. Nevertheless, clients' descriptions of 'being helped' were so graphic that the variables identified helped the researcher to focus and shape the design of an empathy education programme for registered nurses. Variables critical to empathy were as follows:

a)　　　　the need to create an interpersonal climate where it is possible for an empathised awareness of the other person to occur at some point;

b)　　　　the need for helpers to listen to, focus on, and explore the common recurring concerns, or themes expressed by the other person, in the context of the here and now;

c)　　　　the availability of a wide range (repertoire) or responding strategies, and variations within each strategy, so that helpers can cope with the varying degree of clinical difficulty presented by clients;

d)   the possibility that the empathic process can be stalled at any phase if the helper consistently fails to listen, or is consistently clumsy or threatening.

Numerous behaviours relevant to each variable were identified from clients' descriptions of nurse-client relationships. All behaviours described by clients were allocated to either variables a, b or d. All descriptions of positive behaviours were considered to be relevant to variable c because they offered nurses a range of responding strategies. Since all of the client statements were matched with a variable, the validity of the variables was confirmed.

Clients' statements were sorted into two key themes: helpful and unhelpful interpersonal behaviours. This revealed what clients wanted, or did not want, during relationships with nurses. Assertions mentioned by twenty or more clients (66%), which were made at least once, were identified by the researcher and two teaching colleagues. This process resulted in total agreement among raters. All client data was validated against views in the published literature.

The issues identified from these data, when matched with the experience of teaching colleagues and views in the professional literature, formed the basis of the development of an item pool for the empathy scale. Twelve items were developed for the scale that were considered to reflect clients' descriptions of helpful and unhelpful behaviours. Each item was relevant to one or more of the variables considered to be critical to empathy. Since the item pool reflected clients' perceptions of their relationships with nurses, the instrument was considered to measure what Cormack (1985) refers to as the unique use of interpersonal skills in nursing.

The empathy scale comprised the following items:

Item 1   :   Attempts to explore and clarify feelings.
Item 2   :   Leads directs and diverts.
Item 3   :   Responds to feelings.
Item 4   :   Ignores verbal and non-verbal communication.
Item 5   :   Explores personal meaning of feelings.
Item 6   :   Judgmental and opinionated.
Item 7   :   Responds to feelings and meaning.
Item 8   :   Interrupts and seems in a hurry.
Item 9   :   Provides the client with direction.

Item 10   :   Fails to focus on solutions/does not answer direct questions/lacks genuineness.

Item 11   :   Appropriate voice tone, sounds relaxed.

Item 12   :   Inappropriate voice tone, sounds curt.

The twelve items on the empathy scale consisted of six high empathy items, and six low empathy items. That is, six items that were regarded as being helpful in terms of building the empathic relationship, and six items which if overused were likely to impede the development of empathy and the therapeutic relationship. The relationship of items on the new empathy scale to clients' views about helping is discussed in the next section. The investigation of the scale for reliability and validity is discussed in section 4.3.

4.2.3.1 The relationship of the empathy scale to clients' views about helping The relationship of items on the empathy scale to clients' views about helping is illustrated by comments selected from the client sample referred to in section 4.2.3. Discussion of clients' views about helping reveals a relationship between their descriptions of effective and ineffective interpersonal behaviours and variables critical to empathy. Positive scale items (effective behaviours) are discussed first.

Item 1 on the empathy scale (Attempts to Explore and Clarify Feelings) is an example of the extent to which the helper is attempting to listen actively. Clients' descriptions of the early phase of their relationship with nurses indicated that sensitive understanding, or accurate perception on the part of the nurse, was not apparent at that point. However, their comments indicated that nurses' attempts to listen determined whether this was going to happen at some later point in the relationship. Client statements supporting this conclusion included:

> "It is very hard for her to understand me, but she is
> trying very hard."
> And
> "Nobody understands me, but she listens very well."

Item 3 on the scale (Responds to Feelings) reflects clients' need for nurses to be sensitive to their feelings. Clients indicated that this was also critical during the early stages of a new relationship. For example:

> "I don't know her very well, she is very thoughtful. She doesn't object to my thoughts and tries to understand my feelings and reasons."
> And
> "She helped me by listening to me. I find it hard to talk
> or express my feelings, but it is easier talking to her."

Item 5 (Explores Personal Meanings of Feelings) relates to the need for nurses to help clients to clarify their often confused messages by providing more detail about their emotional experiences. Clients' descriptions of this behaviour were congruent with the outcome from Heine's (1950) study, which asked clients which therapist characteristics accounted for therapeutic change. The therapist's response which these clients found most helpful was that the therapist clarified and openly stated feelings which the client had been approaching hazily and hesitantly. This is emphasised by the following client statements:

> "It is not like getting your brains picked. She helps me to let it flow out."
> And
> "It is like speaking to myself or looking into a mirror. She helps me to explain the reasons for my distress."

Item 7 (Responds to Feelings and Meaning) relates to clients' need for nurses to help them to 'anchor' accounts of problems in the personal time and setting of the problem. When that help was provided they were able to move from the general to the particular, from the past to the present. Examples included:

> "He helps me to get to the point and helps me to
> look at the current situation."
> And
> "My doctor always wants to drag up the past, but she is
> interested in what I am like today."

Item 9 (Provides the Client with Direction) reflects the need to help clients to focus on solutions to problems. The response is an example of Peplau's (1984) suggestion that nurses should assist clients to find solutions to personal problems in a manner that reflects their preferences. Client statements supporting that view included:

> "We talked about my current difficulties. She understands my point of view and how upset I am and what I would like to happen."
> And
> "She worked with me on my problems. With my agreement she approached the charge nurse to get me needed information."

Item 11 (Appropriate Voice Tone, Sounds Relaxed) relates to the client's view that nurses ought to sound committed (warmth) and open (genuine). Clients suggested, as Rogers (1957) did, that the communication of these attitudes can help to establish an interpersonal climate of respect, neutrality and trust. The following statement indicates the consequence of a lack of warmth and genuineness.

> "He sounds as if he would rather be in the pub having
> a pint than listening to my rubbish."

This statement indicates that item 11 is crucial in determining the extent to which verbal inputs are judged to be warm. Several client statements suggested that the empathic process could be stalled at any phase of the relationship. The origin of negative scale items (ineffective behaviours) stemmed from their descriptions of threatening behaviours.

Item 2 on the scale (Leads, Directs and Diverts) is an example of manipulating communication. This is illustrated by the following example:

> "She is very clever. I don't want to talk about myself, but she judges what I say and I find that we are talking about me. This is not comfortable."

Item 4 (Ignores Verbal and Non-verbal Communication) refers to the helper's inability to listen. Clients suggested that when nurses failed to hear their communicated message, they felt that nurses did not care. For example:

"She failed to understand how I felt about my condition.
I felt that she did not care."

Item 6 (Judgmental and Opinionated) measures the extent to which the helper is judgmental. Clients suggested that this threatening behaviour damaged the emotional quality of the relationship. For example:

"If someone criticises me or doesn't respect me, I just clam up."

This finding is similar to the outcome from Dittes (1957) research. Using a physiological measure, the psychogalvanic reflex, to measure the anxious or alerted reactions of the client, Dittes correlated the deviations on the measure with judges' ratings of the degree of warm acceptance and permissiveness on the part of the therapist. It was found that whenever the therapist's communicated attitudes changed even slightly in the direction of a lesser degree of respect and acceptance, the number of abrupt GSR deviations significantly increased.

Item 8 (Interrupts and Seems in a Hurry) reflects clients' dislike of being interrupted. For example:

"She didn't give me time to explain. It felt as if I didn't matter."

Item 10 (Fails to Focus on Solutions) reflects a lack of acceptance. Clients suggested that this conveyed the impression that the nurse was not taking them seriously. For example:

"We haven't discussed my problems yet. I am not sure whether she believes me."

Item 12 (Inappropriate Voice Tone, Sounds Curt) reflects clients' dislike of an unfriendly helper. The following client statement illustrates this point.

"I felt defensive because she sounded so hostile."

It was concluded that nurses need to select interventions that are appropriate to the phase of the relationship and the needs of the individual client receiving help. Client statements suggested that under certain circumstances it would be appropriate to explore feelings, coping strategies and health goals. For example:

"I can talk freely to her, there is not a problem."
And
"She can be trusted. You can talk to her about things you would be reluctant to talk to other people about."

However, some clients indicated that at a certain phase of the relationship, in - depth probing might threaten them. For example:

"At interview times I feel panic because feelings are brought to the surface that I would sooner forget. However, she seems to sense this and is supportive."
And
"When I don't want to talk about something she seems to recognise this mood and asks me about it. She won't persist if I am reluctant."

These statements suggest that a repertoire of intervention strategies must be available to the nurse in order to cope with the varying degree of clinical difficulty. Selection of the range of items for the empathy scale considered the need for a range of interventions that were appropriate to the circumstances of the individual client receiving help. For example, if a client signals a reluctance to discuss feelings, the nurse might not find exploration of the personal meaning of feelings (Item 5 on the empathy scale) very productive. An alternative approach which might be more appropriate, would be to say, "Talk about what is comfortable for you at this moment". That is an example of helping the client to clarify the meaning of their communication by providing more detail about their emotional experience (Item 1 on the empathy scale). It differs from item 5 because it allows clients to continue to feel accepted, but able to make choices, when talking about feelings or problems is not comfortable.

The positive items on the empathy scale were considered to reflect the definition of empathy used in this study (see Section 1.3). The presence of a central focus and feeling with and in the client's world is illustrated by items 1,3 and 5, which are dependent on item 11. Accurate perception of the client's world is emphasised by items 7 and 9. Negative scale items signify a lack of empathy as defined by La Monica (1981).

4.2.4 Phase 3: Scoring the empathy scale

The initial item pool was developed into a Likert Scale for the purpose of scoring the instrument. This resulted in an individual's attitudes and behaviours being expressed as a series of numbers, and provided an opportunity to obtain summated scores for the instrument.

A seven-point Likert Scale was developed. Thus, respondents were being asked to choose one of seven statements that reflected best their perceptions of themselves, or another person, on each of the twelve items on the scale. These were: always like, nearly always like, frequently like, quite often like, occasionally like, seldom like and never like. For high empathy items, scoring ranged from a high score of 6, for always like, to a score of 0 for never like. The scoring procedure was reversed for low empathy items. This enabled more precise information to be obtained about the respondent's degree of agreement, or disagreement, which Oppenheim (1992) suggests is a major advantage of Likert Scales over a simple agree/disagree score.

While Oppenheim (1992) points out that most investigators have used a five-point scale, rather than a seven-point scale, he expresses no personal preference for either. However, Polgar and Thomas (1988) suggest that while conventional five-point Likert scales allow for a middle, undecided response, this has the disadvantage of allowing an acquiescent response. While a seven-point Likert Scale also allows a middle response, it is possible that the greater number of points might 'dilute', or reduce, the acquiescent response. Additionally, the researcher's experience of interpersonal relations, suggested that the quantitative dimension of empathy could not be described adequately within the more usual five-point scale. It was felt that empathy was best reflected by an extended Likert-Scale because very few behaviours 'always' happen, or 'never' happen. The features of a user's manual for the empathy scale are discussed later.

4.2.4.1   User's guide to the meaning of scale items The users' manual consisted of i) scoring instructions ii)detailed operational definitions of each item, and iii) clinical examples of each item on the empathy scale. The operational definitions and clinical examples were selected from audiotaped records of clinical interviews (n=100) conducted by registered nurses who had been supervised by the researcher's colleagues during clinical work and developed by the researcher.

The process of content analysis involved the study of clinical interviews in order to identify operational examples of empathy scale items. Operational definitions were then developed by the researcher for each item on the scale. Conclusions about operational definitions were examined by teaching colleagues who were considered to be subject experts. They agreed with the researcher's definitions. Finally, clinical examples of items on the scale were selected for the user's manual. The clinical examples of items on the empathy scale were not intended to be a comprehensive list, but were intended to guide users' understanding of scale items.

4.2.5 *Summary of the development phases*

In this section, it has been shown that:

a)   clients' descriptions of their relationships with nurses helped identify several variables which determined whether they experienced empathy;

b)   these were: (i) an interpersonal climate where it is possible for an empathised awareness of the other person to occur at some point, (ii) exploration of recurring themes expressed by the client, (iii) a wide range of responding skills, (iv) the avoidance of threatening responses;

c)   behaviours relevant to these variables were described by clients and contributed to the generation of items on the new empathy scale;

d)   clients wanted nurses to:
i)   attempt to listen;
ii)   be sensitive to feelings;
iii)   seek clarification of confused messages;

  iv) help them to 'anchor' accounts of problems in the personal
    time and setting of the problem;
  v) help them to focus on solutions to problems;
  vi) sound warm and genuine;
e)   clients did not want nurses to:
  i) manipulate their communication;
  ii) fail to listen to them;
  iii) sound judgmental;
  iv) interrupt them;
  v) fail to accept them;
  vi) sound unfriendly;
f)   positive behaviours (I-VI) reflect Items 1, 3, 5, 7,9 and 11 on
    the empathy scale, negative behaviours (I-VI) reflect Items 2, 4,
    6, 8, 10 and 12 on the empathy scale;
g)   the development of the item pool into a Likert Scale provided a
    means of investigating the effectiveness of a new empathy
    course;
h)   the user's manual guided scorers of the empathy scale.

4.3   Results: The features of the scale that enable nurses to know when they are showing empathy

In this section, it will be shown that:

a) the empathy scale is orientated to what clients want from nurses during interpersonal relationships;
b) in addition to guiding scorers of the empathy scale, the user's manual can guide those who teach empathy.

4.3.1 *The important features*

An important feature of the empathy scale is that it is client centred. Since items on the scale measure behaviours considered to be helpful or unhelpful by clients, this assessment tool measures what clients want from nurses, and is compatible with the aims of the empathy course. The contribution of clients ensured that the item pool was grounded in the natural world, i.e. representative of nurses' relationships with clients and significant others. The scale is compatible with La Monica's (1981) definition of empathy because it is concerned with initiating supportive interpersonal communication.

A construct of empathy that is orientated to what clients want from nurses during interpersonal relationships will enable them to know when they are showing empathy. Additionally, the scale provides nurse educators with information about empathy skills needed by nurses.

A further feature of the empathy scale was the provision of a user's manual which specified how ratings of scale items were to be madeThe aim was to ensure the reliability of the scale by addressing Bergin and Garfield's (1971) and Marshall's (1977) suggestion that scale reliability could be improved if authors specify in adequate detail how ratings are to be made. The provision of such detail is likely to reduce measurement error.

4.4 Evaluation: The new measuring scale is reliable and valid

This section examines the evidence that the empathy scale is reliable and valid. Questions asked about validity included:

a)   the extent to which items on the scale reflected all questions that could be asked about empathy (face/content validity);

b)   the extent to which performance on the new scale correlates with performance on another measure of empathy (concurrent validity);

c)   the extent to which there is a relationship between scores on the new empathy scale and the ability that it is intended to measure (construct validity).

Questions asked about reliability included:

a)   the extent to which there is a correlation between nurses' scores on the empathy scale, on two occasions, over a 2-4 week period (test-retest reliability);

b)   the extent to which all scale items were measuring empathy (internal reliability);

c)   the extent to which all scale items discriminated between people scoring higher on the scale from those scoring lower on the scale (internal discrimination);

d)   the extent to which all trained raters could discriminate consistently between high and low empathisers (inter-rater reliability).

The development and testing of the empathy scale involved examining the scale for reliability and validity. Validity is reported first because that represents the sequence of investigations. The initial investigations of the scale were concerned with face/content validity, concurrent validity and construct validity.

The first investigation was concerned with face validity. The scale items were examined independently by a panel of experts (n = 6) in Rogerian theory. Five were drawn from nursing and one from clinical psychology. All of them utilised Rogerian theory in their clinical work, education, or research. The expert panel adopted two approaches in order to establish face validity.

First, they were invited to comment on the extent to which the items on the empathy scale related to items on La Monica's (1981) Empathy Construct Rating Scale. They did this by listing on a sheet of paper any item on the ECRS, which in their view, was similar to an item on the researcher's empathy scale.

It was not the intention to establish that the empathy scale developed for this study was a direct match with the ECRS. The aim was to identify the extent to which a new scale, developed for the researcher's purposes, contained some of the ideas within the ECRS. This was important because La Monica's definition of empathy, used in the development of the ECRS, was an influence in the development of the new empathy scale.

A majority of the expert panel paired 75% of the items on the ECRs with items on the new empathy scale. Statistical analysis of the raw data by a non parametric test (Kappa Statistic, k) revealed that the probability of this outcome being a chance occurrence was very low (p<0.0001).

Additionally, the expert panel were asked to comment on whether the items on the empathy scale were indicators of empathy. All members agreed that all items on the scale were indicators of the presence or absence of empathy. The two approaches described here established the face validity of the instrument.

It could be suggested that the empathy scale had content validity because it reflected the objectives of the empathy education programme. However, it could still be asked: "To what extent do these objectives reflect all of the questions that might be asked about empathy?" The expert panel were invited to comment on that question during their examination of the item pool, and the content of the users' manual for the scale. No further additions were made to the item pool following this. However, the experts did propose some modifications to the wording of some scale items and some operational definitions of scale items in the users' manual. These modifications were made. It was concluded that the instrument represented adequately the range of questions that could be asked about empathy. This established content validity for the scale.

In this instance the rational and empirical source of the content stemmed from the observations and experiences of the researcher and expert panel. A serious objection to the face or content validity approach is that it tries to defend the fact than an instrument is valid in an either /or sense. Arguably, validity is a characteristic which an instrument possesses to some degree, and does not either have or not have. Content validity is limited to the extent that it does not provide any evidence of the extent to which the instrument is valid. In contrast, other methods of establishing validity express validity as a correlation against some other criterion for the variable being studied. These methods, which include concurrent and predictive validity, are sometimes referred to as criterion-related validity. They are generally considered to be more objective ways of establishing validity (Schalk-Thomas, 1990).

A common approach to establishing concurrent validity is to show the extent to which performance on a new instrument correlates with performance on an existing measure of the characteristic under study. This approach is only defensible if the already existing measure is valid, and is a measure of a different kind from the new one. Because the Empathy Construct Rating Scale (La Monica, 1981) met both of those requirements, the approach described here was adopted to investigate the concurrent validity of the researcher's empathy scale with the ECRS.

Thirty four registered nurses were invited to rate themselves on the new empathy scale and the ECRS under similar circumstances. The strength and direction of the relationship between subjects' scores on the two instruments were examined by the Pearson product moment coefficient (Pearson r). The computed correlation coefficient was 0.85 (p<0.001). This tells us that the new empathy scale and the ECRS were measuring a similar construct.

Construct validity is usually established over time by several people, instead of the originator of the instrument. It is used to explore the relationship of an instrument's results to measures of the underlying theoretical concept(s) of the instrument (Gronlund, 1981).

Gough (1984 - personal communication) confirmed this view when he stated that: "...one way to conceptualise scales and tests in psychology is to view them as tools for identifying persons in whom a quality, talent, or predisposition is likely to occur". Thus a common approach to establishing construct validity is to study new situations where two or more groups can be hypothesised as being different. For example, we can hypothesise that high scorers on an empathy scale will be perceived as being better listeners than low scorers.

Some theorists have suggested that correlating results from an instrument with that of others believed to measure the same construct, is also a method of establishing construct validity. That view was expressed by Johnstone et al. (1983) who repeated an investigation of the Hogan Empathy Scale, conducted by Grief and Hogan (1973), which sought to determine the relationship of the scale with other measures of personality. Johnstone et al. tested the scale for construct validity by correlating results obtained from the scale with 16 different personality tests believed to measure the same construct. Correlations confirmed the unique psychological meaning of the Hogan Empathy Scale, a measure of trait empathy, or empathic disposition.

Messick (1989) reaffirmed correlational analysis as a major approach to construct validation, indicating that different measures of the same construct should converge or be correlated. Arguably, the high correlation between the scores of 34 subjects on the ECRS, and the new empathy scale (r = 0.85), is encouraging in respect of the construct validity of the new scale.

Reliability is usually defined as the ability of an instrument to yield consistent results (Treece and Treece, 1982), or the extent to which measurement error is minimised (Nunally, 1972; Polit and Hungler, 1983). Without sufficient estimates of the reliability of the measures used in a study all results of that study must be viewed with caution. Approaches to the estimation of the reliability of the empathy scale involved the investigation of i) test-retest reliability, ii) the internal consistency among items on the scale, iii) the internal discrimination of scale items, and iv) inter-rater reliability.

Test-retest reliability involves producing two sets of data by administering an instrument once, and then after a period of time, administering the instrument to the same subjects a second time (the retest). The period of time should be long enough for forgetting to take place, but not so long that change could be expected to occur (Fox, 1983).

The test-retest reliability of the scale was investigated by inviting 32 registered nurses to use the instrument over a 2-4 week period of time. Estimates of reliability were obtained by correlating the two sets of data using the Pearson product moment coefficient. The correlation coefficient was .90 ($p<.001$).

In this instance, the time period selected was considered appropriate because the construct being measured, self-reported, state empathy, was not expected to change very much in the subject being sampled. Previous research (Reynolds, 1986) found that self-reported state empathy does not change significantly among measures when subjects are not receiving empathy education. None of these subjects was receiving empathy education at the time of testing.

Internal reliability, or consistency, is concerned with the homogeneity of the data collection instrument. The research question being addressed is the extent to which all items on the scale focus on appropriate concepts. Fox (1983) identifies several ways of coming up with an index of internal reliability.
These include:

a)   computing an estimate of reliability based on the observed correlations or covariances of the items with each other;

b)   correlating the results from two alternative forms of the same test, or splitting the same test into two parts, and examining the correlation between the two parts.

The former approach was chosen to investigate the internal reliability of the empathy scale by computing a reliability coefficient called Cronbach's Alpha. Alpha avoids the limitations of the split half approach where reliability is related to the length of the measure and the exact point where the scale is split. Cronbach's Alpha is based on the average correlation of items within a scale, if the items are standardised. This is appropriate to the empathy scale (a standardised scale) which has been carefully constructed with reference to its objective and to the subject group on which it was intended to be tried out.

The empathy scale is based on the assumption that all items on the scale are positively correlated with each other because they are measuring a component of a common entity, i.e. empathy. The assumption that all items on the empathy scale were measuring a common entity was explored by asking 103 registered nurses to score themselves on the instrument. Cronbach's Alpha for the scale was calculated. The reliability coefficient was .90. The extent to which individual items affect the reliability of a scale can be examined by calculating Cronbach's Alpha when each item is removed from the scale. Calculation of Alpha when each item was deleted from the scale revealed that the removal of any single item would not significantly increase the reliability of the scale. Consequently, all items on the scale were retained at that point (See Appendix 2).

The next investigation involved the internal discrimination of the scale. In this instance the research question is concerned with the extent to which individual items discriminate between people higher on the scale from those lower on the scale. This is an important dimension of reliability because it answers the question: "To what extent do the scores of high and low empathisers go in the right direction on each item?". For instance, according to the theory underpinning the construct, it is likely that high empathisers would attempt consistently to explore and clarify feelings (item 1 on the scale), but would not consistently divert a person from areas of concern (item 2 on the scale). If those items failed to segregate high empathisers from low empathisers, they could be considered to be unreliable indicators.

The internal discrimination of the empathy scale was investigated, statistically, by a correlational test called Phi coefficient. Investigation of the internal discrimination of the scale involved examining the scores of 103 registered nurses who had scored themselves on the instrument. The top third and the bottom third of the scores of nurses for each item, and the total scores for the instrument, were retained for analysis. Phi was calculated by correlating the top and bottom groups' scores with each item with the top and bottom scores for the entire instrument.

The question being addressed by Phi, was the extent to which there is an association between items in the scale and overall scores on the instrument. Values of Phi suggested that all items in the scale segregated high scorers from low scorers (See Appendix 3). Values varied from a perfect correlation of 1 for item 4, to a lower correlation of .68 for item 9. Most values ranged from around .80 and above. The significance level for these correlation coefficients was p<.0001.

Item 9 (providing direction) had an acceptable and significant correlation with the instrument r = .68. However, because it has the weakest correlation of all items in the scale, the item needs to be investigated further when the instrument is not being used as a self-reporting measure. At this point (pre-main study), because item 9 described a helping behaviour that was not covered by any other item, it was retained in the item pool.

A further approach to reliability that should be considered is inter-rater agreement. This is appropriate to situations where two or more raters collect data by observing the same phenomena. If raters are trained and instructions for making ratings are clear, the correlation between scores (inter-rater reliability) should be high. This opportunity presented itself during the main study when raters were trained to rate nurse subjects on the empathy scale from audiotaped records of counselling work.

Prior to and following the main study of a new empathy course three raters rated several taped nurse-client verbal interactions simultaneously, and independently. The resulting records were used to establish the degree of inter-rater reliability.

Polit and Hungler (1983) point out that the training of raters is a crucial phase in the preparation of a study and should not be neglected. Raters must be familiarised thoroughly with the aims of the study, the nature of the behaviours to be assessed, the sampling strategy, and the formal instrument.

Training began with a discussion between the researcher and the raters about the purpose of the observations to be made. The individual items on the empathy scale and the operational definitions were examined and discussed in order to achieve a mutual understanding of their meaning.

When it was felt that a common understanding of the twelve scale items existed among raters, they were invited to rate independently an audiotaped record of a nurse-client counselling interview using the rating scale in Appendix 1. The total scores obtained from three raters (on a range of 0-72) were:

Rater 1 52
Rater 2 56
Rater 3 51

An examination of the results on an item basis revealed that all three raters scored item 1 and 9 on the scale differently. Two raters achieved agreement on nine of the remaining items, while the remaining rater scored those items one point differently on the Likert Scale. With the remaining item, two raters agreed, while the third rater scored two points differently. Inter-rater reliability was calculated at that point (among paired raters) with a percent agreement. The following formula was used:

$$\% \text{ Agreement} = \frac{\text{Number of Agreements}}{\text{Number of Agreements \& Disagreements}} \times \frac{100}{1}$$

The results of this estimation, and the extent to which raters disagreed, is demonstrated by Table 1:

Table 1 First estimation of inter-rater reliability

	Total Agreement	1 Box Difference	2 Box Difference	3 Box Difference	% of Total Agreement
Rater 1 and 2	3	8		1	25%
Rater 1 and 3	4	6	2		33%
Rater 2 and 3	3	7	2		25%

A discussion was then initiated among raters about how they had approached the task of scoring the instrument. This led to further discussion about the meaning of specific scale items. Next, raters scored a fresh subject from an audiotaped record of a nurse-client counselling interview. The total scores obtained from the three raters were:

Rater 1 25
Rater 2 29
Rater 3 24

While inter-rater reliability was not considered to be satisfactory at this point, both results indicated that raters were generally operating at the same end of the scale and recognised subjects of high or low empathy. However, on this occasion raters achieved total agreement on only two items. On eight items, two raters agreed, while the third rater scored one point differently on the scale from the other two. On items 11 and 12, two raters agreed, while one rater scored two points differently from them. The percentage agreement among paired raters is demonstrated by Table 2:

Table 2 Second estimation of inter-rater reliability

	Total Agreement	1 Box Difference	2 Box Difference	% of Total Agreement
Rater 1 and 2	7	5		58.3%
Rater 1 and 3	4	6	2	33%
Rater 2 and 3	5	5	2	41.25%

In view of this result, a discussion was initiated about how the raters has gone about the task of rating the nurse subject on tape, particularly in relationship to items where inter-rater agreement was poorest. Two problematic items related to voice tone (items 11 and 12). On listening to the tape again, raters were able to achieve consensus. It was concluded at that point that part of the difficulty in achieving agreement related to the inexperience of one rater in assessing audiotaped interview data. It was felt also that there was a need to agree on a standard approach towards rating items on the empathy scale. Following discussion between the researcher and raters, agreement about a common approach to scoring the instrument was reached.

First, raters would study all utterances made by the nurse and patient. This decision was influenced, in part, by studies which demonstrate that the judgment of empathy is influenced by the unit of measurement. For example, Mintz and Luborsky (1971) found a lack of correlation between ratings based on segments of a therapy session and the whole session. It was concluded that brief segment measurement of empathy might not be sufficient for accurate judgment of empathy during a counselling interview. Next, it was agreed that for positive items on the scale raters should study the client's current and antecedent behaviour in order to determine the most appropriate response that should have been selected from the repertoire of positive items on the empathy scale. For example, if a rater judged that a client offered two opportunities to provide direction (item 9) and the nurse accepted both opportunities, then the rater would score the subject as Always Like (100%) on that item. On the other hand, if the subject failed to respond to both verbal cues, the rater would score the subject as Never Like (0%), on the scale.

For negative scoring, raters agreed to examine every negative utterance made by the subject. These utterances would be categorised in respect of negative items on the scale (e.g. leading, directing, and diverting, or ignoring verbal and non-verbal communication). Next, raters would score subjects on negative items according to the frequency of specific negative items within the total number of utterances.

The most problematic items were those relating to voice tone (items 11 and 12). These items has been included because several studies suggest that when people interpret verbal communication, more of the variance is accounted for by voice tone than by the content of verbal utterances (see Argyll et al. 1970; Kunst-Wilson et al. 1981). However, raters' comments suggested that scoring voice tone appeared to be more dependent on evaluative dimensions in the rater's mind (for example, good/nice) than any other items on the scale. It was agreed among raters that evaluation of voice tone should be judged in relationship to the observed impact on the client's responses to the nurse. Additionally, scoring of positive voice tone should be the reverse of negative voice tone. For example, if the rater scored item 11 (appropriate voice tone) as Always Like (100%), it followed that item 12 (inappropriate voice tone) should be scored as Never Like (0%).

Following the training day, raters were asked to rate five fresh tapes, independently. Only the third and fifth tapes were used to examine inter-rater reliability. The rationale for this was that the influence of fellow raters would be removed, and that raters would benefit from further practice, while concentrating fully on all five tapes. The total scores obtained from the raters for the third tape were:

Rater 1 52
Rater 2 53
Rater 3 54

In this instance all three raters achieved agreement on four scale items. With the remaining eight items, two raters achieved agreement, while one rater scored one point differently on the Likert Scale from the other two raters. The percentage agreement among paired raters is demonstrated by Table 3:

Table 3 Third estimation of inter-rater reliability

	Total Agreement	1 Box Difference	% of Total Agreement
Rater 1 and 2	7	5	83%
Rater 1 and 3	4	8	33%
Rater 2 and 3	9	3	75%

The total scores obtained from the raters for the final tape were:

1st Rater 29
2nd Rater 31
3rd Rater 32

An examination of those results on an item to item basis revealed that all three raters achieved agreement on seven scale items. With the remaining 5 items, two raters agreed, while the other rater scored one point differently on the Likert Scale from the other two raters. The percentage agreement among paired raters is demonstrated by Table 4:

Table 4 Fourth estimation of inter-rater reliability during the training of raters

	Total Agreement	1 Box Difference	% of Total Agreement
Rater 1 and 2	11	1	91.6%
Rater 1 and 3	8	4	66.6%
Rater 2 and 3	7	5	58.3%

The final inter-rater reliability estimate (pre-main study) was considered by the researcher and his supervisors to be satisfactory for several reasons. First, a review of the literature on the inter-rater reliability of empathy scales revealed that the new empathy scale, developed for this study, was capable of reliability coefficients that were equal to two other popular measures of cognitive-behavioural empathy. For example, Truax and Mitchell (1971) presented a list of inter-rater reliabilities (from 40 studies) that ranged from 42 to 95%, for the Truax Accurate Empathy Scale. Rogers (1967) had, earlier, reported even less encouraging reliability coefficients. In respect of La Monica's empathy scale, Reynolds (1986) reported inter-rater agreements ranging from 46 to 93%.

While there was not total agreement among paired raters on the new empathy scale on all items, where differences existed, they only amounted to a single point (box) on a seven point Likert Scale during the final estimation of inter-rater reliability. An examination of the outcome reveals that rater training resulted in a tendency for raters' scores on the empathy scale to converge during training. This outcome does not suggest that raters' scoring was random.

Inter-rater reliability was investigated further following the post-course study of subjects' empathy scores during a new empathy course (see Chapter 5). This was done following analysis of all audiotapes of clinical work from subjects in a control and experimental group. All three raters were invited to rate, independently, the final tape that was to be analaysed. The total scores obtained from the three raters were:

Rater 1 44
Rater 2 45
Rater 3 42

In this instance all three raters achieved total agreement on five items. With the remaining items, two raters agreed, while the remaining rater scored one box differently on the Likert Scale. The percentage agreement among paired raters is demonstrated by Table 5:

Table 5 Final estimation of inter-rater reliability following main study of subjects' empathy

	Total Agreement	1 Box Difference	% of Total Agreement
Rater 1 and 2	11	1	91.6%
Rater 1 and 3	6	6	50%
Rater 2 and 3	5	7	41.6%

Examination of these data indicate that inter-rater reliability had remained fairly stable. While total agreement among paired raters had declined slightly since training, where differences existed, they only amounted to one point (box) on the seven point scale. This suggests that raters were unlikely to have been using a random criterion for scoring the instrument, during the study of subjects' ability to offer empathy, which is reported in Chapter 5.

A summary of the outcomes of the investigation of the reliability and validity of the new empathy scale reveals that:

a)   the empathy scale represented adequately all questions that could be asked about an ability to show empathy and 75% of scale items reflected items on the Empathy Construct Rating Scale (face/content validity);

b)   the highly significant correlation between performance on the new scale with performance on the Empathy Construct Rating Scale establishes the scales concurrent validity;

c)   the evidence supporting the scales concurrent validity supports the view that there is a relationship between the instrument's results and the ability that it is intended to measure (construct validity);

d)   the high significant correlation between nurses' scores on two occasions, establishes test-retest reliability for the scale;

e)   the evidence that all scale items were measuring empathy, establishes the scales internal reliability;

f)   the evidence that all scale items discriminated between high and low empathisers established the internal discrimination of the scale;

g)   evidence that all trained raters were operating closely together at the same end of the scale, established that an adequate amount of inter-rater reliability existed.

4.5 Summary of the scale for measuring empathy

In this chapter, the need to develop a client-centred empathy scale had been defended. It has been argued that there is a need to find an operational definition of empathy that is relevant to clinical nursing. It is suggested that clients' perceptions of their relationships with nurses clarify the meaning of the construct of empathy in nursing. The development of the new empathy scale, and user's manual, provides a means of enabling nurses to know when they are offering empathy.

The investigation of the new empathy scale for reliability and validity was satisfactory. Nevertheless an important question is the extent to which raters were measuring empathy, or something else. The empathy scale used in this study was developed and tested in order to overcome such criticism. Measures taken included the development of operational definitions for scale items, and the provision of a users' manual. This was intended to ensure that accurate interpretation was possible. As indicated earlier a method of scoring the Likert Scale was established which involved raters studying all utterances made by the nurse and client. Scoring the instrument was not just based on what the nurse has said, but on the most appropriate response to the client's current and antecedent behaviour. The rigour of training provided for raters, and the approach developed for studying all utterance events, during the entire clinical interview, were likely to reduce the possibility that raters were measuring something other than empathy. Additionally, inter-rater agreements demonstrate that all raters were able to discriminate easily between high and low empathisers, as measured by the scale.

The items on the empathy scale used in this study had many of their antecedents in clients' perceptions of helpful and unhelpful relationships. This suggests that not only are those items relevant to clinical nursing but that they can be defined (Reynolds, 1994). If clients can perceive and identify the nuances and effective components of interpersonal relationships, then it ought to be possible to train professionals to recognise them. This suggests that subjects' test scores during this study were an accurate interpretation of what was actually happening during the nurse-client relationship. This conclusion suggests that the empathy scale is valid.

5 Solution, Part 2: Using this scale, a course has been developed which does help nurses to show empathy

In this chapter, the need for an effective way of teaching nurses to show empathy, and research questions relevant to that aim, are considered. The development of an empathy course for helping nurses to show empathy and the features of that course are described. The results of the investigation of the research questions and the evaluation of the effectiveness of the course, are presented in the final part of the chapter.

5.1 Need: For an effective way of helping nurses to learn how to show empathy

In this section, it will be shown that:

a) there was a need to devise an effective way of helping nurses to show empathy in clinical contexts;

b) there was a need to understand whether nurses' attitudes to their education prevent them from showing empathy;

c) there was a need to investigate which components of empathy education affect nurses' ability to offer empathy;

d) there was a need to understand which variables in nurses' clinical environment affect nurses' ability to offer empathy.

Concerns about existing empathy courses (see Chapter 3) related mainly to the extent to which they could influence the ability of nurses to offer empathy in the real clinical world. Even when courses did provide a supervised clinical component, there was no evidence that the learning outcomes could be replicated in clinical nursing, because those courses did not involve nurses. There was a concern that training gains might not be sustained in clinical environments which were not supportive of clinical empathy. There was doubt about whether learning outcomes, reported in some nursing studies, reflected an ability to offer empathy. Doubt arose from the tendency to rely on subjective impressions of learning, rather than blind ratings from trained observers on instruments that measure the qualities or behaviours assumed to be relevant to the clinical work of nurses.

In view of the lack of evidence in the research literature that experiential workshops had influenced clinical nursing, it was logical to suggest that educators need to devise ways of helping nurses to offer empathy in clinical contexts. This was indicated by the suggestions in the literature (e.g. McKay et al., 1990) that major barriers to clinical empathy existed in nurses' clinical environments. Barriers to empathy may include the way in which nursing work is organised traditionally, and a fear of risk taking when the client's emotional distress is too overwhelming (Hughes and Carver, 1990).

Theories of situated learning (Lave and Wenger, 1991) suggest that nurses require assistance to study the construct of empathy during the reality of relationships with clients, in the real clinical situation, where it will be applied. For this reason the design of the course reported later in this chapter includes a clinical component. Clinically focused empathy education is likely to be more meaningful because it challenges teachers to assist students to study the impact of their behaviour on the behaviour of the client. This is important because, as Haggerty (1985) has noted, many nurses do not identify positive client outcomes resulting from their verbal interactions and therefore lack immediate feedback about the effectiveness of nurse-client communication. Guttman and Haase (1972) suggest that such feedback is likely to make learning more meaningful, because knowing about empathy becomes relevant to practice, and this is likely to reinforce the retention of empathy skills in the clinical area.

The discussion, thus far, has raised questions about variables that may influence nurses' ability to offer clinical empathy. There were no clear answers to these questions, and so three research questions were identified and investigated by this study. These investigations were a phase of the development of a course to help nurses to show empathy because they contributed to an understanding of what affects nurses' ability to learn how to apply empathy to clinical nursing (see section 5.4). This phase occurred after the course was developed and piloted. The research questions were:

a) does anything in nurses' attitudes to education prevent them from learning to show empathy?
b) which components of empathy education affect nurses' ability to show empathy?
c) which variables in clinical environments affect nurses' ability to show empathy?

5.1.1 Question 1: Does anything in nurses' attitudes to education prevent them from learning to show empathy?

Numerous contributors to the literature suggest that nurses do not show much empathy to clients (Melia, 1981; McLeod-Clark, 1985; Mackay et al., 1990), so it is possible that nurses' own attitudes prevent them from learning to show empathy. In spite of the frequently stated view that the nurse-client relationship is a problem-solving relationship, in which the aim is to increase the client's satisfaction with living (Reynolds and Cormack, 1990; Chambers, 1994; O'Toole and Welt, 1994), nurses generally may not share that view.

An additional consideration was the possibility that nurses' attitudes to education may prevent them from utilising learning styles that are productive but unfamiliar. This point is emphasised by Duncan and Biddle (1974) who suggest that prior experience of education results in preconceived ideas about learning that influence students' attitudes to other ways of learning. This suggests that students on the empathy course that is the focus for this study may not be receptive to the learning process offered. For this reason, it was considered necessary to investigate nurses' attitudes to education, as well as their reasons for undertaking an empathy course.

5.1.2 Question 2: Which components of empathy education affect nurses' ability to show empathy?

Unfortunately, the literature reveals that nurse educators do not know how best to help nurses to offer empathy, and how to transfer classroom learning to clinical practice (Mackay et al., 1990). We cannot be certain what accounted for training gains during previous empathy courses, whether learning outcomes were sustained, or whether (often modest) training gains have any clinical significance. This suggested that there was a need to investigate which components of empathy education are critical, in order to extend understanding of how nurses learn to apply empathy in clinical environments.

5.1.3 *Question 3: Which variables in clinical environments affect nurses' ability to show empathy?*

A major concern in the nursing literature is the reported inability to transfer classroom learning to clinical practice. A major theme of the arguments presented by all authors is the extent to which nurse-training programmes fail to prepare students to show skills necessary to facilitate the resolution of problems experienced by clients (Bregg, 1958; Altschul, 1972; Wisser, 1974; Cormack, 1976; Wong, 1979; Macilwaine, 1980; Kreigh and Perko, 1983; Clinton, 1985; Reynolds, 1986; Chambers, 1990; Bishop, 1994). This criticism has been particularly strong in respect of nurses' ability to detect and manage the psychosocial needs of clients (Melia, 1981; Cormack, 1983; Faulkner, 1985; Reynolds, 1990; Chambers, 1994).

It has been argued that the differing social contexts experienced by learner nurses in clinical environments influence their opportunity and tendency to implement and reflect upon interpersonal theory during clinical work. Chapman's (1983) observation that in some situations nurses are discouraged from getting involved with the client's emotions suggests that different views exist within the nursing culture about the role and function of the nurse.

If nurses are to develop the necessary skills and attitudes, they need to apply these to practice. Paradoxically the social context of clinical environments may sometimes prevent this from happening. There is a need for nurse educators to be aware of this because there seems little point in offering empathy education unless clinical application of the construct can be guaranteed.

Studies of empathy education programmes for nurses suggest that so far they have not influenced nursing practice as dramatically as expected (Kalish, 1973; La Monica et al., 1987; Reynolds and Presly, 1988; Wheeler and Barrett, 1994). Morse et al. (1992) question the appropriateness of the use of empathy in some clinical settings. This challenge is based on those authors' conclusion that the manner in which nursing is organised acts as a barrier to high-empathy nursing. This view is reflected also by other writers in earlier publications (Griffin, 1983; Gordon, 1987).

The central theme presented by these writers is the extent to which the assumptions underlying a counselling/psychotherapy approach 'fit' with different practice settings and varying client outcomes strived for by different professional groups. According to Morse et al. (1992) a basic assumption which underpins a counselling approach is that:

> the empathetic relationship occurs within a professional counselling context. The counsellor has uninterrupted time to establish a therapeutic one-to-one relationship and sees the client on a regular basis until counselling goals are achieved (p 277).

Morse et al. (1992) argue that empathy is not possible in acute medical/surgical settings because workload does not usually give a nurse the time to spend 30 minutes or longer listening to one client. Furthermore they suggest the nature of client assignment in these settings does not ensure continued contact, and the nurse-client relationship is usually terminated when the client is discharged, often within 10 days.

The evidence cited so far suggests that the organisational context of clinical nursing, which may be influenced by staffing levels, ward environment, and the clinical problems of clients, might be a major influence on the nature of nurse-client verbal interactions.

5.1.4 Summary of questions arising

In this section, it has been shown that:

a) concerns about whether previous empathy education have enabled nurses to show empathy to clients in practice, indicate a need for an effective way of teaching nurses to show clinical empathy;
b) nurses require assistance to study the construct of empathy during the reality of relationships with clients;
c) research questions generated as the final phase of the development of an empathy course were concerned with variables that may affect nurses' ability to offer empathy; these variables were i) nurses' attitudes to

education, ii) effective course components and iii) nurses' clinical environments.

5.2 Method: Phases of development of an empathy course for helping nurses to show empathy

In this section, it will be shown that:

a) phases of the development of the empathy course included i) reviewing the literature and ii) reviewing teachers' experiences of teaching interpersonal skills;

b) a distance learning course was developed to teach nurses to offer the interpersonal conditions measured by the client-centred empathy scale and piloted with groups of registered nurses;

c) nurses' attitudes to education were investigated by semi-structured interview before they commenced their empathy course, and following education;

d) the effectiveness of components of the empathy course were investigated by semi-structured interview 3-6 months after the course;

e) the extent to which variables in clinical environments affected nurses' ability to offer empathy was investigated by pre- and post-course interviews, and a context-of-care questionnaire, administered during the clinical component of the empathy course;

f) investigation of the interview and questionnaire methods revealed that they were reliable and valid.

5.2.1 Overview of development phases

Three phases were used in developing the empathy course. Each phase is discussed in greater detail later in this section.

Firstly, the researcher reflected on personal experience and the literature relating to how empathy is learned. This was done in order to devise an effective way of helping nurses to show empathy in clinical contexts.

Secondly, a course was developed and piloted with registered nurses in various clinical specialties. This was done in order to enable teachers to familiarise themselves with the features of the empathy course.

Finally, variables that may affect the ability of nurses to offer empathy were identified from the literature and subsequently investigated. This was done in order to find out whether certain variables placed a constraint on nurses learning how to offer empathy and to identify which course components were effective. The research questions were investigated at the same time as the investigation of nurses' ability to offer empathy, reported in section 5.5.

5.2.2 Phase 1: The origins of a course to teach nurses to offer empathy

Existing courses had clearly not helped nurses to show empathy during clinical work so it was concluded that there was a need to develop a way of helping nurses to learn how to offer clinical empathy. The empathy course subsequently developed, originated from the researcher's accumulated teaching, clinical and research work, and from principles of educational design.

Experience of teaching interpersonal relations in classrooms and nurses' clinical areas provided insights into the difficulty of transferring classroom learning to clinical practice, and emphasised the need for a course that provided an opportunity to practise empathy in the real training situation (Reynolds, 1982; Reynolds and Cormack, 1990). An impression was gained that students' experiences during clinical work become an increasingly rich source of learning, and that students wish to learn about topics that are relevant to their own world. The assumptions arising from that experience were reinforced by the literature on adult education (Knowles, 1980) and the opportunity to work with experts in educational approaches that were intended to teach students to learn how to learn (e.g. Novak and Gowan, 1986).

Experience from a previous study of student nurses' empathy suggested the need for a more structured approach to teaching empathy (Reynolds, 1986). The outcomes of that study indicated that there was no preparation for clinical work, very little attempt to provide clinical practice, and varying degrees of contact with educators who introduced students to the topic. The concerns about these findings were reinforced by the limitations of existing empathy courses, reported in Chapter 3.

All experiences gained over a decade were reviewed with colleagues experienced in teaching the interpersonal aspects of nursing. A view emerged that there was a need for an empathy course which would assist nurses to learn from the study of their own clinical practice. The content and design of a new empathy course evolved from these discussions. At this time it was recognised that there was a need for a measure of empathy that quantified nurses' ability to offer empathy in clients' terms. This was achieved (see Chapter 4). A course was developed to teach nurses to offer empathy in clients' terms which included many elements of distance learning. The new course was piloted with groups of registered nurses. The experiences gained by teachers enabled them to learn how to support learners on the course.

5.2.3 *Phase 2: Decisions taken about the development of a distance-learning course to teach nurses how to offer empathy*

While the features of the empathy course are discussed more fully in the next section (5.3), the distance learning mode is discussed here because the decision to use a distance learning approach was a phase of the development of the course. The need for distance learning was indicated by the fact that many potential students worked in areas remote from the main study centre. Access to education was difficult for many nurses due to the cost and time involved in travelling, and restricted transportation, particularly during winter.

The solution developed was to provide each student with a teacher who would travel to students' locations in order to provide face-to-face contact, and one-to-one supervision. Students on the course were encouraged also to contact their personal supervisor by telephone and fax, and when possible, by e-mail or video conferencing. The distance learning method developed, allowed students to fit part-time education around work and family commitments and reduced the problem of access to education caused by distance. The only course component which required students to attend the study centre was a two-day workshop.

The provision of regular one-to-one supervision of clinical work is atypical of distance learning. However, the provision of a self-directed study pack and the opportunity for students studying at a distance to meet as a group, are typical elements of distance learning programmes (Robinson and Shakespeare, 1995).

5.2.4 Phase 3: Finding answers to the three research questions

The research questions were investigated by a pre-course and post-course interview (see Appendix 4) and a context-of-care questionnaire (see Appendix 5). The interviews were conducted by the researcher immediately before nurses in an experimental group commenced the empathy course developed for this study, and 3-6 months after the course. The context-of-care questionnaire was administered to nurses in the experimental group immediately following clinical work with a client.

5.2.4.1 Interview method used to answer Question 1 The first research question was:

> Does anything in nurses' attitudes to education prevent them from learning to show empathy?

This question was investigated by all questions on the pre-course interview schedule and Question 1 on the post-course interview schedule. The selection of questions for the pre-course interview was influenced by Duncan and Biddle's (1974) model of learning. These authors suggested that any examination of the effectiveness of education needs to take account of pre-course variables, process variables (during education) and the outcomes of education. The aim of the pre-course interview was to explore properties that nurses were bringing into education and their formative experiences. Formative experiences of learning are likely to contribute to attitudes towards education. Attitudes are context variables to which teachers must adjust. The questions, and the rationale for questions used to investigate the first research question, can be examined in Appendix 6.

5.2.4.2 Interview method used to answer Question 2 The second research question was:

> Which components of empathy education affect nurses' ability to offer empathy?

This question was investigated directly by question 2 on the post-course interview schedule. It was anticipated that the remaining two questions on the post-course interview would provide further insights into nurses' reasons for considering some course components to be more effective than others. The selection of questions for the post-course interview was influenced by Duncan and Biddle's (1974) view that there is a need to investigate what influences learning (process variables) and the long term effect of learning (outcome variables). The questions and the rationale for questions used to investigate the second research question can be examined in Appendix 6.

5.2.4.3 Survey method used to answer Question 3 The third research question was:

> Which variables in clinical environments affect nurses' ability to offer empathy?

This question was investigated by the third question on the pre- and post-course interview, relating to barriers to learning, and a context-of-care questionnaire. The context of care questionnaire was administered to nurses following the fifth supervised clinical interview in a series of six, which was a component of the empathy course. The rationale for the items on the questionnaire can be examined in Appendix 6.

Before administering the interviews and survey methods, the instruments were investigated for reliability and validity.

5.2.4.4 The reliability and validity of the interview method The methods utilised to ensure that interviews obtained the same results again and again (reliability), involved:

a)   scrutiny of interview questions by supervisors and colleagues to determine the extent to which they could be understood by respondents;

b)   studying the responses of a group of nurses on the empathy course to determine whether any questions were ambiguous;

c)   examination of pilot interviews by a qualified rater for interviewer bias and variation of response to interviewees;

d)   interviewing all subjects under the same circumstances;

e)   inviting two raters to examine audiotaped records of pilot interviews in order to investigate the reliability of the coding system established for data analysis.

It was revealed that questions were understood by respondents, that the interviewer was objective and that all subjects were being asked questions in an identical manner. In respect of the coding system, raters agreed with the researcher's categories on more than 95% of occasions, suggesting that concepts identified by the researcher were supported by the data obtained from interviewees.

The methods utilised to investigate the extent to which the interview was measuring what it was intended to measure (validity), involved:

a)   the selection of questions which reflected the variables in a specific model of learning (Duncan and Biddle, 1974);

b)   comparison of the researcher's interpretation of the interviewees' utterances with the interpretations of the interviewee and an independent rater. All raters' independent interpretations were similar on more than 90% of occasions;

c)   establishing rules for coding during content analysis which involved the development of themes representing the content of interviewees' utterances and the identification of specific concepts within each general theme. Thus, the researcher firstly assigned content to a general theme and then identified specific events and feelings within the general theme.

5.2.4.5   The reliability and validity of the survey method   As with the interview schedules, care was taken to avoid ambiguous questions. The initial draft questions, which originated from teachers' experiences, were reviewed by supervisors and teaching colleagues for clarity. Next, the questionnaire was piloted with students on the empathy course (n = 18). As a consequence of doing this, some questions were reframed because they were not eliciting an appropriate or detailed response.

The revised version was piloted with twenty nurses on the empathy course. Responses in all cases were appropriate, specific, and fairly detailed. It was concluded that the questions were being understood clearly by the respondents.

In terms of the research environment, the importance of completing the questionnaire immediately following the clinical interview, to avoid memory lapse and bias, was emphasised. All respondents were able to do this during the pilot study, thus controlling an important influence on the reliability of the instrument.

The face and content validity of the instrument lie in the origins of the questions. The questionnaire and the responses elicited were scrutinised by teaching colleagues. They concluded that the questions represented the universe of questions that could be asked about the context of clinical practice during the empathy course. These issues were familiar to them from their experiences of supervising students on the course.

The richness and candour of the responses suggested that the questionnaire was valid. The detailed and specific descriptions of impediments to learning, and personal feelings about difficulties, encouraged the view that these data described reality. This impression was confirmed by similar data obtained from post-course interviews with nurses who had completed the questionnaire.

The final validity issue involved the approach toward developing the rules of coding data. A naive coder was invited to initiate a coding system for data obtained from the pilot study of the instrument. The coding system developed was based on her knowledge of the English language, and owed nothing to preconceived ideas of the phenomena being studied. This strategy reduced the potential limitation of professional bias, or a prior view, to some extent. It was possible to let the data speak for themselves. Weisberg and Bowen (1977) refer to this method as the contextual approach where a coder identifies the categories that the respondents actually use and employs them in the coding scheme.

Scrutiny of the coding system developed by the naive coder by the researcher and colleagues, suggested that numerous categories known to exist in clinical environments had been identified from these data. However, it could still be asked whether the categories within the coding system were exhaustive. By that is meant, the extent to which every answer to the questions fits into one of the categories. A professional research assistant was invited to examine both the coding system and the data. While the second rater did not disagree with any categories identified by the naive coder, she did add some new categories to the coding system, thereby increasing its scope to be exhaustive.

5.2.5. Summary of development phases

In this section, it has been shown that:

a)   the new empathy course has its origins in the literature and the combined research and teaching experiences of the researcher and teaching colleagues;

b)   due to the problems of distance from the main study centre, an empathy course was developed that contained many of the features of distance learning;

c)   the new course was piloted with groups of registered nurses in order to provide teachers with an opportunity to understand the needs of students and to develop ways of assisting them to learn;

d)   questions relating to variables that may affect nurses' ability to offer clinical empathy, were investigated prior to, during and following nurses' experience of a course designed to teach them to show clinical empathy;

e)   nurses' pre- and post-course attitudes to empathy education, and perceptions of effective course components (post-course), were investigated by semi-structured interview;

f)   variables in clinical environments that may affect nurses' ability to offer empathy were investigated by a context-of-care questionnaire, immediately following a fifth clinical interview, and then by a post-course interview;

g)   the interview and survey methods were found to be reliable and valid during pilot studies.

5.3   Results: Features of the empathy education course for helping nurses to show empathy

The extent to which the findings from the research questions supported the need for the empathy course that was developed, is discussed in the next section (5.4). The components and process of this course, which will now be described, were intended to facilitate open, non-defensive learners who could review their ideas and experiences objectively.

5.3.1 Components and process of the empathy course

The training programme consisted of several components. These were:

a)   a self-directed study pack with activities that increasingly focus the student's attention upon events in their clinical practice;

b)   wider literature searches;

d)   regular one-to-one meetings with a supervisor, scheduled by the student, for the purpose of reflection on theory and practice;

e)   a two-day workshop prior to clinical work where simulated practice and group discussion occur. This is for the purpose of preparing the student for practice in the real clinical world;

f)   supervised clinical work. This consists of a supervised review of six (audiotaped) clinical interviews in the student's practice area;

g)   a measure of cognitive-behavioural empathy which reflects course aims. This instrument is used to focus workshop activity and supervised review of clinical work. It is included in the self-directed study pack where an early activity invites students to reflect on the meaning of scale items.

While the nature and amount of course work is determined by teacher-student assessment of an individual's needs, the common route through course work is demonstrated by Figure 2.

Figure 2 Students' route through course work

Day 1	Introduction to coursework
Initial 5 weeks	During this time students help develop the one-to-one supervisory relationship, work with the study pack and review literature.
End of week 5	2 day workshop for all students to prepare for clinical work.
Week 6 to completion (Week 9)	Activity consists of supervisory review of clinical data and reflection on all coursework with supervisors. During this time students also develop their essay assignment.

Prior to the two-day workshop, students work through a self-directed study pack which is introduced to them during an introductory day to the course and the learning method. During the initial five weeks they also read wider literature. The focus for literature searches is related to topics associated with the sections in the study pack. For example, the therapeutic significance of empathy, operational definitions of empathy, and so on. During this time, student-initiated contacts with their supervisor (one-to-one or telephone) are related to the literature that they are reading and conclusions drawn from activities in the study pack. An example of an early activity is demonstrated in Appendix 11.

5.3.2 The workshop

The workshop occurs towards the end of the initial five weeks of coursework. It consists of activities that are intended to prepare students for clinical work with clients. These activities consist of:

a)   listening to taped segments of nurse-client communication, and then rating the helpers' level of empathy on the empathy scale developed for the course;

b)   listening to segments of client statements, and then formulating high-empathy responses to these statements;

c)   practising empathy during role play and discussing the approach with supervisor and associates.

5.3.3 *Activity during the final weeks of the course*

During the final weeks of the course, students continue to schedule supervisory meetings which are focused on wider reading and activities in the study pack. However, during this time supervisory sessions are focused also on a review of six audiotaped clinical interviews, and essay drafts. The clinical work requires students to:

a) make a contract with a client for one or more counselling interviews;

b) agree with the client about the method of recording the interview;

c) schedule a post-clinical conference with a supervisor, immediately following each counselling interview;

d) Transcribe parts of the interview prior to supervision and utilise items on the empathy scale to critique the progress of the clinical interview.

During the supervised review of students' clinical work they are encouraged to study the clinical data from audiotaped records of their counselling work. The focus for supervisory review is the relationship between many elements in the client's narrative. From this position student and supervisor are able to consider the general flow of the conversation, regularly occurring themes and the impact of the language of the nurse upon the language of the client. This approach is intended to enable students to develop their repertoire of the responding skills which build the empathic relationship.

5.3.4 *Time spent on coursework*

The course was designed for nine weeks duration, but the actual amount of time and its distribution was negotiated between an individual student and the supervisor.

This course differs methodologically from previous courses. It consisted of a background of distance learning, in addition to which the nature and function of the supervisory relationship is viewed as being a critical component of students' personal growth. This view stems from

Rogers (1969, 1977) approach to education which evolved from his earlier theoretical formulations about the nature of counselling and personality development. According to Rogers, individuals are capable of being creative, trustworthy, forward moving and realistic, when they are free of defensiveness. He suggests that these capacities will be released in a relationship that has the characteristics of an open, two-way, critical reasoning relationship. Reynolds (1985) alluded to this point when he stated that: *"A permissive, democratic supervisory structure will promote learning more effectively than an authoritarian structure in which students are given directives"*.

For this reason the amount of course time was flexible since individuals require different amounts of time to build a relationship which has as its purpose the promotion of student reflection on theory and practise. This is a process which Novak (1991) calls metacognition. Teachers also need time to assess what students know, understand how they learn, and to respond effectively to dynamics operating within the supervisory relationship which may impede learning. Such dynamics include apathy, anxiety and low self-confidence (Bandura, 1977; Reynolds, 1990).

Unlike earlier nursing studies, where practical application of the construct occurs in classroom environments, the training programme required that students practise in both the classroom and clinical area. In this way the research study associated with the programme was intended to have value for the realities of the training situation. Bandura (1977) argues that it is possible to give the individual experience of successful outcomes by prolonged and graded exposure to the training situation. The empathy training programme described here is intended to provide students with graded exposure to empathy, from the theoretical to simulated laboratory work, and finally by introducing students to clinical work. This approach is similar to the training provided by Carkhuff and Truax (1965). In the study pack the student is introduced to clinical and research knowledge concerning cognitive-behavioural empathy. Experiential (classroom) learning is then provided, which requires students to rate their ability on the empathy measure used during this study from taped nurse-client interactions. Finally, students role-play and their clinical interviews with clients are taped and reviewed.

This approach differs from teaching programmes which emphasise interpersonal techniques. Students are not being taught techniques directly, or being encouraged to memorise rigid 'canned' responses. What is expected is that students will be able to vary their response when necessary, and that these responses are underpinned by a cognitive and theoretical understanding of the clinical issues. As Peplau (1987) suggests, *"The outcomes of counselling have a lot to do with the attitudes and theoretical beliefs of the counsellor about how, and under what conditions people change themselves in favourable directions"*.

5.3.5 Content of the empathy course

The content of the training programme was related to Rogers' (1957) theory of non-directive counselling. The full theoretical content can be examined in a self-directed study pack, which is one component of the course (Reynolds, 1989). The study pack consists of six sections, each of which contains subsections. The contents of each section can be examined in Appendix 11.

5.3.6 The aims of the empathy course

The aims of the empathy course are reflected in the items on the empathy scale (see Chapter 4). The scale is used to assess the extent to which nurses offer the interpersonal conditions favoured by clients.

In this section, it has been shown that:

a)   the empathy course required that nurses practice in both the classroom and clinical area;

b)   it is designed to provide nurses with graded exposure to empathy, from the theoretical to simulated practice, and finally to introduce nurses to clinical work;

c)   audiotaped records of clinical work enabled student and supervisor to consider the general flow of the conversation, regularly occurring themes and the impact of the language of the nurse upon the language of the client;

d)   the empathy scale is used to critique the progress of the clinical
           interview.

5.4   Answers found to the research questions

In respect of answers to the research questions, it will be shown that:

a)   prior to their empathy course, nurses were generally motivated
           to improve their inter-personal skills, but they had little
           awareness of what their course entailed;
b)   pre-education, several nurses wanted guidance from an
           empathic supervisor who would assist them to learn from their
           own experiences and interpersonal relationships;
c)   post-education, nurses viewed learning outcomes positively,
           describing many of them in terms that were similar to items on
           the client-centred empathy scale;
d)   the most effective course components were i) self-judgment of
           clinical ability by reviewing transcripts of clinical interviews,
           ii) an open, two-way, non-defensive supervisory relationship,
           and iii) direction with clinical work;
e)   barriers to offering clinical empathy include: lack of time,
           clinical problems of clients, interruption to clinical work and
           lack of support from unsympathetic colleagues.

This section reports the findings from the investigation of the
three research questions. The extent to which the results support a view
that empathy can be taught and learned, or whether the results introduce a
constraint to that outcome, is considered.

Data obtained from the pre- and post-course interviews, and the
context-of-care questionnaire provided answers to the research questions.
Content analysis of interview data involved the development of themes
representing the content of the interviewee's utterances and the
identification of concepts (specific events) within each general theme.
Due to the large number of concepts generated within most themes, only
concepts mentioned by at least 30% of subjects are discussed in this thesis.

Concepts mentioned by fewer than 30% of subjects are briefly commented on if they provide insights into the most commonly occurring concepts.

Answer 1: Nurses' attitudes to education

The first research question was:

> Does anything in nurses' attitudes to education prevent them from showing empathy?

This question was addressed by the first two questions on the pre-course interview and the first question on the post-course interview. Data obtained from this investigation can be examined in Appendix 7.

The outcomes of this investigation revealed that most nurses were aware (pre-course) of the need to improve their interpersonal skills and were motivated to do so (Table 15). This was in spite of the fact that some nurses (25%) had little awareness of the concept of empathy and most did not know what coursework involved (Table 16).

Prior to education, most nurses expressed a preference for learning from their own experiences and a credible supervisor who would provide them with guidance when needed. Some nurses required access to an empathic supervisor who would provide a safe relationship (Table 18). Following empathy education, nurses perceived the course to be effective and provided graphic descriptions of how they were able to offer empathy to clients(Table 20). An example was an ability to explore the meaning of feelings and experiences. These descriptions were very similar to observations of trained raters during these nurses' actual clinical work (see section 5.5). Several nurses acquired an operational definition of empathy (Table 21). These data do not suggest that nurses' attitudes to education impeded their ability to learn how to offer empathy.

Answer 2: Effective and ineffective course components

The second research question was:

> Which components of empathy education affect nurses' ability to show empathy?

This question was addressed directly by the second question on the post-course interview. The outcomes of this investigation can be examined in Appendix 8.

Data revealed that the nature of the supervisory relationship and reflection on clinical experience were considered to be the most effective course components. The most frequently mentioned concepts in relation to supervision were an open, two-way, non-defensive relationship with a supervisor and direction with clinical work (Table 23). Reflection on clinical work was facilitated by students' review of audiotaped records of their clinical interviews with clients (Table 24). This method, referred to in the literature as Interpersonal Process Recall (Kagan, 1990), was considered to be the most effective course component. While many other course components were perceived to be effective, Interpersonal Process Recall was considered to be more relevant to learning how to offer empathy than other ways of learning (see Tables 26 and 27).

Answer 3: Barriers to empathic behaviour in nurses' clinical environments

The third research question was:

Which variables in clinical environment affect nurses' ability to show empathy?

This question was investigated by the third question on the pre- and post-course interview schedules and the context-of-care questionnaire.

This investigation consisted of two parts: i) nurses' perceptions of barriers to empathy prior to education, and ii) barriers to empathy observed during the clinical component of the empathy course. The outcomes of these investigations can be examined in Appendix 9.

The conclusion from these investigations is that nurses' anticipation of barriers to offering empathy in their own clinical environments (pre-course) was justified (see Table 29). A challenge to offering empathy is presented by variables existing in clinical areas. Important variables are lack of time (n=8/20) and the clinical problems of clients (n=9/20)(see Tables 31 and 51). Further variables are: lack of privacy (n=10/20), interruption to clinical work (n=13/20) and lack of support from unsympathetic colleagues (n=10/20) in circumstances where the skills mix is inadequate (n=7/20). Clinical interviews often occurred in circumstances where privacy (n=10/20) and comfort (n=7/20) could not be guaranteed (see Tables 34 and 36). While data displayed in Appendix 10 demonstrates differences among clinical environments, only six nurses reported freedom from distraction. Sources of distraction included background noise (n=6/20) and interruption by clinical staff (n=3/20) or other people (n=2/20) (Table 35). While eight nurses reported that colleagues had no effect on the interview, six of them avoided the effect of clinical associates and poor skills mix by conducting the interview in their own time (see Tables 38 and 52).

All of these variables have the potential to prevent the nurse from listening to clients and understanding their needs. This is indicated by the fact that most nurses (n=17/20) varied the planned length of the interview (see Tables 39 and 40). Furthermore, while nurses were able to formulate objectives (n=20) and to identify clinical problems of clients (n=19/20) (see Tables 41 to 43), they seldom described clients' needs in terms of specific health outcomes desired by their clients (n=15/20) (Table 44). The explanation may be that many nurses had limited experience of their client at the time of the fifth clinical interview (see Tables 45 to 48). Most nurses experienced tension and/or self doubt (n=19/20) as a consequence of the barriers to offering empathy (see Tables 32, 49 and 50). This may act as a further barrier to empathy. Barriers to learning were most commonly overcome by seeking supervisory support (n=16/20) (Table 33). These findings should be noted by educators who offer a course intended to teach people how to offer empathy in clinical environments.

In this section, it has been shown that:

a)   while nurses' attitudes to education did not place a constraint on learning to show empathy, nurses' clinical environments may impede the ability to offer empathy;

b)   variables in nurses' clinical environments which affect nurses' ability to show empathy can result in nurses feeling anxious, having limited experience of a client and influence the duration and focus of the clinical interview;

c)   the most important components of the empathy course are:

d)   reviewing transcripts of clinical interviews;

e)   an open, two-way, non-defensive supervisory relationship;

f)　　　　　direction with clinical work.

5.5　Evaluation: The new empathy course is effective according to the new measuring scale and other measures as well

In this section, it will be shown that:

a)　　　　　the new empathy scale was administered to investigate nurses' ability to offer empathy prior to education, during education and following education;

b)　　　　　scores on the empathy scale from different measures were compared;

c)　　　　　nurses in the experimental and control groups were observed interviewing real clients, or a simulated client in order to present the same test to a number of nurses;

d)　　　　　statistical analysis of nurses' test scores were intended to show whether the groups were similar or different on any occasion;

e)　　　　　because there was no significant effect of real or simulated clients on empathy scores, the influence of type of client can be disregarded, and data from different real clients can be treated as equivalent;

f)　　　　　there was no significant difference between the empathy scores of the experimental and control groups, prior to education;

g)　　　　　during and following empathy education, the experimental group showed significant gains in empathy scores, while the control group did not change significantly;

h)　　　　　the experimental group obtained percentage gains on all items on the empathy scale during education, and retained most of that gain post-education, while the control group did not change very much;

i)　　　　　several outcomes of education which were reported by subjects during a post-course interview were similar to items on the empathy scale;

j)　　　　　the most effective part of the empathy course was interpersonal process recall which was facilitated by the review of audiotaped records of nurses' clinical interviews;

k)   the course's effectiveness depends on nurses' supervisors acting in an empathically supportive role.

The new empathy scale and the post-course interview provided a means of investigating the effectiveness of the empathy course. The questions probed by analysis of scores on the empathy scale were:

1.   do nurses entering the education programme possess well developed empathy?
2.   does the empathy education programme enable participants to become more empathic?
3.   how long-lasting are the effects of the empathy education programme in respect of nurses' scores on the new empathy scale?

The design of this investigation included:

1.   the measurement of nurses' empathy prior to empathy education, during education and post -education;
2.   the measurement of a control group's empathy at the same time as subjects in the experimental group.

The empathy scale was used by trained raters to rate nurses 'blindly' in experimental and control groups from audiotaped records of their clinical interviews with clients. The experimental group were registered nurses who were receiving empathy education and were recruited from a variety of clinical specialities. The control group consisted of registered nurses who had not received and were not receiving formal empathy education. The two groups were matched in respect of several characteristics - clinical experience, gender, education and age. The matched groups ensured as far as possible that a statement about cause-effect relationships could be made.

These data were collected over a one-year period from nurses who completed one of two empathy modules offered that year (n = 22), and from the control-group subjects (n = 15). Simulated and real clients were used for this investigation. Half the nurses in both groups were rated against a simulated client and half against real clients on three occasions (see figure 3).

Figure 3   Overview of data collection points relating to scores on the empathy scale

	Pre-course		During Education (5th clinical interview)		Post-course	
Experimental Group n=22*	SC n=11	RC n=11	SC n=10	RC n=10	SC n=10	RC n=10
Control Group n=15*	SC n=8	RC n=7	SC n=7	RC n=6	SC n=7	RC n=6

SC = Simulated Client   RC = Real Client

*Following pre-course measures two nurses withdrew from each group.

A simulated client was used to present the same test to a number of nurses, to compare the resulting data with data from real clients and thence to decide whether comparisons between data from different real clients could be treated as equivalent. The approach adopted addressed the issue of different levels of clinical difficulty.

Nurses who were invited to counsel a simulated client were confronted by a research assistant trained to model the behaviour of a typical client. The research assistant's training involved a study of three audiotaped records of a simulated client interacting with a registered nurse. These taped simulations were developed by the research assistant and teachers who taught on the empathy course. The aim was to teach the research assistant to present consistently the same level of clinical difficulty to all nurses who were matched against the simulated client.

Data collection was associated during education with the fifth clinical interview of the course in a series of six scheduled interviews. Supervision consisted of a review of the audiotaped records of clinical work using items on the empathy scale as a focus. All nurses in the experimental group had this experience but 50% of nurses were invited also to counsel a simulated client at the time of their fifth clinical interview for the purpose of data collection. Control group nurses were similarly involved but education and clinical supervision were not provided to them.

Data consisted of three empathy scores for each nurse who completed the study. The experimental and control groups each consisted of sub - groups, one of which counselled a real client and one of which counselled a simulated client.

Statistical analysis consisted of:

a)   analysis of variance (one-way independent groups);
b)   analysis of variance (one-way repeated measures);
c)   t-tests for independent samples.

These investigations were intended to answer the questions; are the two groups (experimental and control) different initially as regards empathy scores and are there changes in empathy scale scores over a time period in the groups?

For this study, the level of significance was set at 1% (p<.01). While some writers (e.g. Fox, 1983; Polit and Hungler, 1983) suggest that p<.05 is the minimal acceptable level in social science research, it was felt that a stricter level was indicated in view of the fact that the decisions had important consequences for nurse-client relationships. A stricter criterion reduces the possibility of erroneously rejecting the null hypothesis (a Type I error), Howell (1989) points out that the more stringent the criterion, the more likely it is that the null hypothesis will be accepted when it is false (a Type II error). The selection of the 1% level of significance was a trade-off between those two concerns.

An initial objective of data analysis was to determine whether matching some nurses with real clients had influenced empathy scores. As was suggested earlier, it was considered likely that nurses counselling real clients would encounter varying degrees of clinical difficulty that might influence the outcome of education. The introduction of some nurses to a simulated client provided the opportunity to check that the data from different real clients could be treated as equivalent. The hypothesized relationship between type of client and empathy was investigated by analysis of variance (Table 6).

Table 6   Effect of interviewing real or simulated clients and control / experimental group

Interview	Value of F for		
	Effect	Group Client	Interaction Group v Client
1	0.28	0.12	0.21
2	43.44*	0.11	0.99
3	56.40*	0.17	0.04

* = P<.01 All other differences are NS

ANOVA of each of the three occasions of interviewing revealed no significant effect of client, real or simulated, and no significant interaction between group and client.   Therefore, the influence of type of client can be disregarded and data from different real clients can be treated as equivalent. As a consequence of that finding, the experimental and control groups were each treated as one group during subsequent investigations.

The next investigation examined nurses' average levels of empathy as measured by the empathy scale, prior to empathy education. An initial examination of these data (Table 7) suggested that the scores of the experimental and control groups were similar on this occasion.   This was confirmed by analysis of variance (Table 8).

Table 7   Means and standard deviations for empathy scores prior to empathy education

Variable Label	Mean	Standard Deviation	Cases
Entire sample	29.51	9.48	37
Control group	28.20	9.14	15
Experimental group	30.40	9.81	22

Table 8 Analysis of variance of scores of control and experimental groups on three clinical interviews

Main effect of group	F value	Significance
Interview 1 (pre-course)	.26	NS
Interview 2 (during education)	46.61	p<.001
Interview 3 (post-education)	60.51	p<.001

ANOVA of interview 1 shows no significant effect of group. Because the control and experimental groups were indistinguishable, they could be considered to be well matched samples.

ANOVA of interviews 2 and 3 (Table 8) shows a significant effect of group on empathy scores. Examination of mean scores (Table 9) reveals that the experimental group had gained considerably in their empathy scores during education, while the scores of the control group had remained static. Following education (3-6 months later) the mean empathy scores had declined slightly but the experimental group had maintained its advantage over the control group (Table 9).

Table 9 Means and standard deviations for empathy scores during and following education

Variable label	During Education		Following Education		
	Mean	SD	Mean	SD	Cases
Entire sample	42.45	15.27	38.42	14.91	33
Control group	28.00	7.28	23.61	6.95	13
Experimental group	51.85	11.10	48.05	9.81	20

The difference in mean empathy scores of the experimental and control groups on the three occasions of interviewing were investigated by a t-test (Table 10).

Table 10   t-Test of differences between empathy scores on the first, second and third interviews

Pairs of Interviews	Value of t for group	
	Control	Experimental
1 and 2	0.44	6.84*
1 and 3	2.48	6.01*
2 and 3	1.84	2.22

* p<.01 All other vales are not significant

The t-test between scores on interviews 1, 2 and 3 shows no significant difference for the control group between any pairs. For the experimental group there was a significant change between interviews 1 and 2 and between 1 and 3, but not between 2 and 3. This outcome indicates that there was a difference which persisted and which was due to education.

An investigation of item gains was conducted in order to determine the extent to which each item on the empathy scale had contributed to the outcome. It was anticipated that certain items would be easier to teach and learn than others in the time available for course work.

In order to calculate the percentage gain or loss, a maximum score of 6 was accepted as the denominator against which change would be calculated. In this way the percentage increase, or decrease, has the same meaning. The method of calculating the percentage gain involves:

$$\text{Interpretation 1} = \frac{\text{Occasion 2 score - Occasion 1 score}}{6} \times \frac{100}{1}$$

$$\text{Interpretation 2} = \frac{\text{Occasion 3 score - Occasion 1 score}}{6} \times \frac{100}{1}$$

Means, standard deviations, and maximum/minimum scores were computed for each item on the scale, from measures obtained pre-course (See Table 11). Also, percentage gains, standard deviations and maximum/minimum scores were calculated from measures obtained during education, and following education. The results obtained from the subject groups on those occasions are demonstrated by Tables 12 and 13).

Table 11 Pre-course item scores for experimental and control groups

Item	EXPERIMENTAL GROUP				CONTROL GROUP			
	Mean Score	SD	Max Score	Min Score	Mean Score	SD	Max Score	Min Score
1	1.90	1.21	4	0	2.15	1.52	5	0
2	2.20	1.40	4	0	2.15	1.07	4	1
3	1.80	1.36	5	0	1.54	0.97	3	0
4	2.85	1.31	5	1	2.69	1.32	5	1
5	1.15	0.99	3	0	1.23	0.72	3	0
6	3.20	1.36	5	1	2.85	1.28	5	1
7	0.80	1.00	4	0	1.08	1.11	3	0
8	4.05	1.39	6	2	4.00	1.41	6	2
9	0.35	0.81	3	0	0.15	0.38	1	0
10	3.05	1.28	5	1	2.61	1.20	5	1
11	4.70	1.08	6	2	4.31	1.38	6	2
12	4.70	1.08	6	2	4.31	1.38	6	2

Table 12 Item gains during and following education (experimental group)

Item	DURING EDUCATION				FOLLOWING EDUCATION			
	Mean % Gain	SD	Max Score	Min Score	Mean Score	SD	Max Score	Min Score
1	+ 36.67	26.27	6	1	+ 31.67	26.9	5	1
2	+ 35.00	32.85	6	1	+ 29.17	29.5	6	2
3	+ 34.17	25.64	5	1	+ 25.00	26.2	5	1
4	+ 28.33	26.55	6	2	+ 25.00	23.8	6	2
5	+ 41.67	27.84	5	0	+ 29.17	28.5	5	0
6	+ 25.83	26.75	6	1	+ 25.00	23.2	6	3
7	+ 46.67	29.91	6	1	+ 35.00	26.9	5	0
8	+ 25.00	24.48	6	3	+ 17.50	30.3	6	3
9	+ 26.67	21.90	4	0	+ 19.17	21.8	4	0
10	+ 28.33	24.24	6	1	+ 25.83	24.8	6	2
11	+ 11.67	19.57	6	1	+ 10.00	22.5	6	3
12	+ 11.67	19.57	6	1	+ 10.00	22.5	6	4

Table 13 Item gains during and following education (control group)

Item	DURING EDUCATION				FOLLOWING EDUCATION			
	Mean % Gain	SD	Max Score	Min Score	Mean Score	SD	Max Score	Min Score
1	- 15.38	27.61	2	0	- 14.10	24.39	2	1
2	- 6.41	18.68	3	0	- 8.97	21.10	3	1
3	- 3.85	21.68	4	0	- 7.69	21.10	3	0
4	- 2.56	17.80	4	1	- 6.41	23.11	4	1
5	- 5.13	14.25	3	0	- 3.85	12.08	2	0
6	- 1.28	28.43	4	2	0.00	19.24	5	2
7	- 1.28	17.30	4	0	- 5.13	26.69	4	0
8	- 8.97	33.07	6	1	- 14.10	21.35	6	1
9	+ 1.28	10.68	1	0	+ 2.56	11.48	2	0
10	+ 3.85	23.72	4	2	+ 1.28	23.04	5	1
11	- 8.97	26.89	6	2	- 2.56	17.80	6	2
12	- 8.97	26.89	6	2	- 2.56	17.80	6	2

The initial baseline investigation of group means for each item on the scale provided the opportunity to establish average performance on individual items prior to education. An examination of these data (See Table 11) revealed that, with the exception of item 11 (appropriate voice tone), subjects scored higher on negative items than positive items. The likely explanation for item 11 being an exception is that it is strongly associated with item 12 (inappropriate voice tone). That is, if a subject scores highly on item 12, raters were instructed to rate the subject highly on item 11. With the exception of item 1 (control group), both groups obtained means of less than 2 on the positive items. This finding is of concern to nursing because the items on which nurses scored less well relate to investigative counselling skills. Those skills are needed in order to understand the meaning of the client's experience and to help the client to resolve health-related problems (See Chapter 2). While nurses performed better on negative items, group means revealed that there was considerable scope for training gains on some items that were critical to the development of the empathic process. Those items included the tendency to lead, direct, and divert the client, and the tendency to ignore verbal and non-verbal communication. Such behaviours are likely to prevent the development of an interpersonal climate of trust. These findings suggest that the mean score for the instrument of 29.5, obtained pre-course, is not sufficient for therapeutic helping.

The item gains for the experimental group during education are displayed in Table 12. The experimental group obtained percentage gains on all items, ranging from +11.6% for item 11 and 12 (voice tone), to +46% for item 7 (responding to feelings and meaning). The largest percent gains were obtained for positive items. This is unsurprising in view of the fact that, pre-course, nurses obtained lower scores for positive items than negative items. While these results are encouraging, it should be noted that with the exception of item 11, item 9 (provides direction) obtained the lowest percentage gain (+26%) among the positive items. This item is a critical behaviour because it involves assisting a client to find solutions to personal problems in a manner that reflects the client's preferences. This skill would appear to be the most difficult one to promote during training. This should be of concern due to the extremely low baseline levels of the skill prior to education.

The results obtained from the control group, who received no education, can be examined in Table 13. Small percentage increases were obtained for item 9 (+1.2%) and 10 (+3.8%) during education for the control group. However percentage increases resulting in less than one-point on the Likert scale are not likely to be clinically significant. All other items demonstrated a percentage loss ranging from -1.2% for items 6 and 7, to -15.3% for item 1. Only item 1 achieved a loss of one point on the Likert scale. Generally, changes among item scores in either direction, on the second occasion, were very small and not likely to be meaningful.

The post-education gains for the experimental group, for each item, among the first and third measures can be examined in Table 12. All items displayed a slight percentage loss between occasion 2 and 3 which amounted to less than one point on the Likert Scale. Items 5(-12.5%) and 7 (-11.6%) came closest to achieving a one-point loss. This suggests that those items, involving an active response to the meaning of feelings, may be the most vulnerable to regression once formal training has ceased. Nevertheless, these data can be considered to be encouraging due to the retention of a proportion of the percentage gains achieved between the first and second measures. This indicates that training gains were relatively stable some 12-24 weeks after education.

The post-education outcome of the item scores for the control group can be examined in Table 13. These data reveal that on this occasion items 9 and 10 maintained a small percentage increase over the first measure (pre-course). Item 6 recovered parity with the first measure (+/-0%). All other items displayed a percentage loss among the first and third measure of less than 1 point of the Likert scale. This indicates that in terms of clinical significance the control group had not changed very much between measures. Changes had occurred in both directions and were of a smaller magnitude than losses occurred by the experimental group on the final measure.

An important finding was that the experimental and control groups were well matched samples prior to education. The experimental group's gain in empathy scores during education, which was maintained 3-6 months post-education, was significant. Investigation of item gains and losses confirms the extent to which the experimental group was more empathic than the control group during and following education. The effectiveness of the empathy course is supported also by nurses' descriptions of what they learned during education.

The investigation of the outcomes of education generated one major theme, the development of new attitudes, insights, and skills. This theme was mentioned on 126 occasions and generated most concepts (see Table 19, Appendix 7). Thus in response to the question about the extent to which course objectives had been met, nurses were mainly focused on the extent to which the course had changed them.

In relation to the personal growth of nurses, many of the most frequently mentioned concepts were compatible with items on the empathy scale. An example included exploring the meaning of feelings and experiences, which is roughly analogous with item 5 on the empathy scale. The possible explanation for nurses stating learning outcomes in terms of empathy-scale items is that teachers used the instrument as a focus for supervision, during a review of audiotaped records of clinical interviews. In spite of this concern, the increase of 41% for item 5, reported by trained raters, and the percentage gains observed for all other items, suggest that nurses' perceptions were valid. Nurses' perceptions of change on scale items recording percentage gains suggest that the empathy scale may have shaped their responses during clinical work, as Reynolds and Presly (1987) predicted.

Nurses' descriptions of their clinical work indicated that they were more aware of their personal limitations (n=8/20). Comments about awareness of opinionated behaviour (n=2/20), and avoidance of the client's concerns (n=2/20) are encouraging. This indicates that, at least, some nurses are recognising that the impact of their language on the behaviour of the client can influence the extent to which verbal interactions are therapeutic. As Peplau (personal communication, 1983) has pointed out, students often change their account of clinical work to make themselves look better. The fact that some nurses felt safe enough to be self-critical suggests freedom from defensiveness and greater self-awareness. This indicates a possibility that they are likely to be more open and committed to clients. These responses are similar to Rogers' (1957) concepts of warmth and genuineness.

Recognition of personal limitations is also an example of reflective practice which Reid (1993) defines as a process of reviewing experience in order to learn about practice. Even if the gains obtained on the empathy scale during supervision are not maintained, it is possible that individuals who are reflective, and aware of personal limitations, are likely to be more committed to listening to the client than those who are not.

In spite of the care taken to match nurses in the control and experimental group, an important question is whether the educational intervention will work in another setting and with different nurses. This question relates to external validity, the generalisability of the research findings to other samples. It is often asserted that small sample studies, such as this one, may be generalised only in a limited way (Woods and Catanzaro, 1988). Strictly speaking, the findings of a study can only be generalised to the population of nurses from which a study sample has been randomly selected (Polit and Hungler, 1983). It can be said that the population of nurses available for this study contained many of the typical characteristics of post-registration nursing students in Scotland.

5.5.1 *The most effective part of the course is interpersonal process recall*

The post-course interviews revealed that the most effective course component was the review of audiotaped records of the nurse-client interview (n=19/20). This method is referred to in the literature as Interpersonal Process Recall (IPR). The teaching strategy was originally developed by Kagan (1973) and others to reduce the possibility of bias and distortion during the review of the verbal and non-verbal aspects of the process of helping relationships. Kagan (1990) states that IPR is designed to help students to recognise and act on subtle, pervasive messages between themselves and a client. Audiotaped recording of interviews provided accurate records of what occurred during clinical interviews. It enabled students to record all verbal communication, even when the client spoke rapidly, and to record subtle differences in meanings (nuances) during the interview. An advantage of IPR is that it is impossible for students to fake the data, in order to make themselves look good. Additionally, as Kagan (1990) points out, IPR is the study of and practice in making explicit the mutual impact of counsellor on client.

Nurses suggested that review of clinical data enabled them to know whether their language was constructive or destructive (n=10/20). This perception is compatible with Murphy's (1971) suggestion that students' perception of their effectiveness and clients' expressed reactions are areas which offer more valid evaluation of the effectiveness of the curriculum in the preparation of practitioners. The problem in nurse-client verbal interactions is the ambiguity of the data. As Peplau (1995) suggests, it has to be made more concrete by recording the process in order to look at it. Nurses' descriptions of the review of audiotaped data in Appendix 9 confirmed that something that a nurse says to a client and repeats regularly can facilitate or damage the therapeutic relationship. These data suggested that this can only be detected and learned by recording the interaction and studying the raw data. In view of the fact that the empathy scale was the focus for reviewing clinical data, it is possible that the scale was an important influence on learning. The scale provided a structure for reflecting on the data.

5.5.2 The course's effectiveness depends on supervisors acting as empathically supportive enquirers

The outcome of post-course interviews revealed also that the nature of supervision was critical. This finding supports the views in the literature that nurses can experience problems in translating theoretical concepts into practice unless they are provided with expert clinical supervision (Smoyak, 1990; Brennan, 1993; Peplau, 1994). Various concepts were identified within the theme of supervision. However, these data revealed that the supportive nature of supervision is essential to learning outcomes. The concepts mentioned most frequently related to the non-defensive nature of the supervisory relationship (n=18/20) and direction with clinical work (n=15/20). This finding is similar to Rogers' (1957) view that people can be forward - moving and realistic if they experience a relationship that is free of defensiveness. Less frequently mentioned concepts such as encouragement to reflect on practice (n=10/20), positive feedback (n=7/20), and commitment to the student (n=5/20), reinforced the idea that supervision was a core component of the learning process. The overwhelming conclusion was that supervision needed to be open, two-way and non-threatening, and that it needed to be focused on clinical work. This result is similar to Stockhausen's (1994) findings that the process of reflection on practice allows the clinical facilitator to be an integral component of the student's learning in clinical contexts.

Of great interest to educators are those aspects of clinical supervision which facilitated favourable learning outcomes. The answer seems to be that students learned through self-judgment of their clinical ability by reviewing transcripts of tapes. Recording of verbal and non-verbal aspects (voice tone) enabled nurses to reflect privately on what they knew and how it related to what they were discovering. This ability was released within a supervisory relationship which was supportive and was possible because audiotapes provided the opportunity to capture and study the raw data from clinical work. This approach is compatible with Ausubel's (1963) suggestion that the role of the teacher is a facilitator of learning. The emphasis here would be on a person creating climates, moods and relationships which allow learners freedom should they wish it, or dependence and direction should they need them. These data suggested also that supervisors attempted to help students to link what they knew already to what they were observing. This approach is compatible with Novak's (1990) views on meaningful learning, and Schon's (1987) view of the reflective practitioner. Nurses reported that they were attempting to transfer learning from one supervisory session and apply and study it during the next interview, which indicates that the learning process is an example of both reflection in action and reflection on action. This approach contrasts with reflection on action which has been utilised for earlier empathy programmes which were classroom based (Dietrich, 1976;

Layton, 1979; La Monica, 1983). The ability to judge when learners want freedom to reflect on experience, or when direction is required, is dependent on an empathised sensitivity to the learner's needs.

5.5.3 *Summary of effectiveness*

a) there was a significant difference between the scores of the experimental group between measures 1 and 2, but not between measure 2 and 3, and no significant differences between any measures for the control group. This indicates that there was a difference in the experimental group, which persisted, and which was due to education;

b) item analysis revealed that the experimental group gained on all items on the empathy scale during education, and retained most of that gain following education, while the control group did not change very much on any scale items;

c) item gains on the empathy scale, reported by trained raters, were confirmed by nurses in the experimental group during descriptions of their learning gains;

d) review of audiotaped clinical work (IPR) was considered to be the most effective part of the empathy course;

e) the effectiveness of the empathy course is dependent upon an empathic supervisor who provides direction with practice, when needed,

f) in view of the effectiveness of the empathy course these findings suggest that an empathy course which does not provide those elements is less likely to be successful;

5.6   Summary of the course for empathy education

In this chapter, the need for an effective way of teaching nurses how to offer clinical empathy has been established. Research questions relating to variables that may affect nurses' ability to offer empathy have been identified. The answers to these questions indicate that the subjects' attitudes to education did not affect their ability to learn how to offer empathy, but numerous variables in clinical environments may impede clinical empathy.

Investigation of the effective components of the empathy course revealed that the most effective feature of the course was Interpersonal Process Recall (Kagan, 1995) in the form of a review of audiotaped clinical interviews. The effectiveness of this method, and the ability to cope with barriers to clinical empathy, is dependent on a supportive supervisor who acts in the role of empathic enquirer.

The empathy course is effective. This was established by significant gains among measures on the new empathy scale for the experimental group. It was established also by the fact that nurses on the empathy course achieved gains on all items on the empathy scale, following pre-course measures, while the control group did not change. Nurses' gains in empathy persisted for some time after the course finished. These outcomes were confirmed by nurses' graphic descriptions of their learning during post-course interviews.

These data indicate that a course which does not include the effective course components reported in this study is less likely to influence the low level of clinical empathy reported in nursing. The findings should interest nurse educators and have implications for the aims of the health service.

6 Summary and implications: Such a course may help others to learn as well

This chapter consists of three parts. First, the implications of the research and development findings for nurse education are considered. Secondly, the implications for the health service are discussed. Finally, future directions for research are identified.

6.1 Implications for nurse education

In this section, it will be shown that:

a) the aims of nurse education ought to be concerned with enabling nurses to offer something different clinically, as well as knowing something different;

b) there is a need to consider what educational experiences need to be provided in order to achieve these aims, and how learning is best organised;

c) in order to achieve the desired outcome of education, teachers need to negotiate protected clinical practice and need to possess clinical skills, as well as an ability to facilitate their students' study of knowledge in clinical environments, within a relationship that is free of defensiveness;

d) there is a need to develop assessment tools which reflect the desired learning outcomes of courses and to train users of such tools, in order to ensure reliable assessment of learning outcomes that education is intended to promote;

e) nurse educators have a responsibility to exhibit empathic behaviours to their students.

Because this study showed that a specific education had an effect, there is a need to consider the implications for the future design of nurse education. The findings indicate clear implications for educational programmes which are concerned with empathy and the broader domain of interpersonal relations. The question which needs to be asked is: "How can nurse educators put the findings into practice?" In other words, what would nurse education look like in the future, if the findings were to be implemented?

The design for nurse education that is proposed by the views emerging from the study will offer its own challenges. Nevertheless, the findings do suggest that if nurses are to overcome the reported theory-practice dichotomy, particularly in relation to interpersonal skills, there is a need for educators to change some of their existing practices. The change in the curriculum, suggested by this study involves the answer to four questions. These are:

a)   what educational aims should teachers seek to attain?
b)   what educational experiences need to be provided to attain those aims, and how should they be organised?
c)   what skills do teachers need to facilitate the desired outcome of education?
d)   wow can we determine whether the aims of education are being achieved?

The findings of this study indicate that nurses were motivated to improve their clinical skills. This suggests that there is no point in education existing unless it results in nurses being able to do something different clinically, as well as knowing something different. While it might seem self-evident that nurse education exists for that purpose, the studies of nurses' interpersonal skills, reported in Chapter 2, reveal that education does not always result in the skills which are necessary to achieve favourable health outcomes for clients.

A major aim of nurse education might be to help nurses to move clients toward their optimum health goals. In order to achieve this, it is essential that education results in nurses recognising the clinical problems of clients which are potentially responsive to some nursing action. The aim is for nurses to focus on problems that nursing is expected to correct, ameliorate, change or prevent. In this way the initial emphasis is not on skills, what nurses do, but on the problems of clients that nurses can treat. From this position, the goal should be to encourage nurses to apply and refine their repertoire of helping skills, unlike teaching programmes which focus on skills alone, the aim being to enable students to judge the efficacy of their approach by observing the effect of their clinical work on the clinical needs of the client.

Relating the context of skills training to clients' problems, and health outcomes, will assist clinicians to understand the relevance of certain nursing actions. Clinicians need to make appropriate clinical decisions when they are working with individual clients.

This suggests a further aim, the need to facilitate nurses' ability to make judgments about the practical usefulness of any theory applied to their practice. Essentially this means that nurses should test their theories against their own practical clinical observations and personal reality.

In order to achieve the desired aims of education, it is necessary that nurse educators consider the following elements of the learning process:

a) the relevance and contribution of College work
   to clinical practice;
b) how to enable students to study their clinical practice;
c) the organisation of clinical practice.

The College of Nursing is unlike the real clinical training situation and for that reason it is arguable that students and teachers should spend as little time there as is consistent with obligations which require them to be in College. Learning involves more than memorising information; it involves the curiosity that drives people to absorb everything that they can see, or hear, in order to improve the efficiency of their performance. This tendency is best released during structured clinical practice. This means that there needs to be a context for the material that confronts students, a reason for knowing something. For example, there is little point in telling a learner nurse that you should not argue with an angry person, unless the nurse is allowed to observe and practise an alternative approach. When that happens, learning is likely to be meaningful and remembered out of sheer necessity, because it may mean that physical violence is avoided.

It is not being suggested that there is no point in students attending the College of Nursing. This study suggests that productive activity can occur in College. Students value, and need time, to do literature searches on topics which they are studying. The College should be used also to enable students to talk to each other. This has the effect of allowing students to learn from the experiences of their peers, and to realise that their struggle to learn is experienced by all students. Time in College allows students to know a teacher who will supervise their clinical practice. Time needs to be provided for one-to-one discussions with that person who should assess what the student already knows.

While it is useful to simulate clinical practice in the classroom, it should be recognised that this activity is only a preparation for clinical work. Theory, clinical issues and related skills, studied in class, should be practised in clinical environments. Ideally, concepts studied in class should be studied immediately in the clinical area.

Skilled clinical supervision by a subject expert is essential if concepts studied in College are to be learned meaningfully. However, educators need to know what skilled clinical supervision involves. The present study indicated that nurses perceived skilled supervision to be a process which enabled them to learn from their clinical data. In order to facilitate students' study of the clinical data, teachers need to possess certain attributes and develop methods of studying what goes on during nurse-client interactions. The skills required by teachers are discussed later. In relation to the study of nurse-client interactions, there is a need for teachers to be present physically in order to study their students' efforts to learn how to apply theory to practice. Alternative ways of capturing the essence of nurse-client interactions may involve audiotaped recordings of the verbal aspects, or flow charts of the decision-making process. While tools are necessary in order to focus on the process of nursing, there is a need for students to discuss their clinical work with teachers close to the moment of practice. Such post-clinical conferences provide the opportunity to review the effect of nursing care on the client's health status, the degree of clinical competence, and the opportunity to understand the student's feelings and perceptions. This is what is meant by skilled clinical supervision.

Clinical practice of concepts studied in College needs to be guaranteed. This requires the recognition that students need to interact with clients in order to make self-judgements of their clinical ability in a context that relates to the client's need for nursing. In order to do this, students need to be provided with a supervisory structure which frees them from the distractions that normally exist in clinical areas. In order to free students from distractions, teachers need to negotiate protected clinical time for the purpose of studying and helping the client. This implies that teachers need to be highly visible in clinical areas in order to ensure that negotiated conditions for supervision are not violated and to observe their students' efforts to learn. By working together on barriers to clinical learning, students and teachers are provided with further time to develop a supervisory relationship that is facilitative. This relationship which may be initiated in the College of Nursing, needs to be tested in clinical environments.

A logical conclusion is that those who purport to teach nursing should also practise nursing. Close supervisory review of interaction data, a process which includes role-modelling and analysis of the clinical data from nurse-client interactions, provides teachers with an opportunity to direct clinical practice and learn with their students. In this way, students can have the confidence that their teacher is competent, and experience a clinical context that is compatible with their theoretical orientation to practice. The best way of establishing the teacher-clinician role is for each teacher to have a small clinical case-load which can be utilised as a focus for their students' practice.

The dual teacher-practitioner role is a method of ensuring that teachers do not become de-skilled, and that their teaching does not become irrelevant to the way in which nursing is delivered. It is also a way of ensuring that the minimal conditions of adequate clinical supervision are delivered. These conditions are:

a) supervisors should possess and practise the clinical skill which is to be taught and learned;

b) supervisors should be capable of facilitating a supervisory relationship which empowers students' ability to learn how to learn and understand the relationship between concepts;

c) supervisors should be familiar with, and competent in, theories of nursing which guide the student's actions and thoughts;

d) supervisors should be visible, approachable, and readily available to the learner when needed.

When teachers accept responsibility for their students' clinical practice, there will be no need to delegate responsibility for clinical supervision to clinical nursing staff who may not be able to teach or have the time for supervision. In some instances, clinical staff may not even be skilled clinicians. This possibility is suggested by the frequent reports in the literature of deficiencies in nurses' interpersonal skills (see Chapter 2).

The skills needed by teachers relate to two themes. These are:

a) the interpersonal nature of the teacher-student relationship;

b) the extent to which teachers can influence students' clinical work.

A critical condition of the teacher-student relationship is that it should be non-defensive. This is necessary in order that students feel free to discuss openly their existing knowledge and to reflect on new experiences and insights. Teacher-responses needed to facilitate an investigate learning climate include:

a)   sensitivity to students' feelings;
b)   commitment to students' learning;
c)   acceptance of students' perceptions;
d)   willingness to share personal knowledge;
c)   honesty.

These attributes are similar to the Rogerian constructs of empathy, warmth and genuineness. Thus, teachers need to possess interpersonal skills, putting their own feelings aside, and consciously imagining themselves in the place of students in order to genuinely understand them. They should be aware also of the powerful influence of their own values and beliefs, while seeking to treat all viewpoints equally. When teachers are able to achieve these conditions they can facilitate student growth. As with the nurse-client relationship, it is the teacher's responsibility to study the dynamics that operate within their relationships with students. This involves studying the nature and variations of the relationships, and from this formulating solutions that will resolve any difficulties which may impede students' learning.

In order to influence students' clinical work, teachers need to provide direction with clinical work, encourage students to reflect on clinical experience, and enable students to be confident enough to apply new learning to future clinical practice. This suggests that, in addition to interpersonal skills, teachers need to possess:

a)   clinical skills;
b)   reflective ability.

Clinical skills are needed in order that teachers' classroom work during workshop situations is realistic. More importantly, these skills enable them to provide their students with direction during clinical work, and to provide them with a role model. In other words, teachers ought to be capable of demonstrating the clinical skills that they expect their students to learn. This point seems as logical as suggesting that violin teachers ought to be able to play the violin.

It is difficult to understand how a non-reflective teacher can facilitate a reflective practitioner (Schon, 1987). Subjects referring to reflection on action, alluded to the extent to which teachers were able to help them to evaluate their observations. This seems critical because reflection involves a major change in thinking. In order to learn how to form good habits of inquiry, students need exposure to teachers who are capable of independent thinking, can draw conclusions that follow logically, and are able to increase the capacity to see things afresh.

Teachers need to make instructional decisions which are based on observation. These data are required to help answer questions such as which students need specific learning experiences and the extent to which students are achieving the minimum aims of a course. While teachers can make informal observations and judgments, measurement and assessment tools provide more comprehensive, systematic and objective evidence on which to base instructional decisions. However, with measurement and assessment tools, certain conditions need to be met. These are:

a) items on assessment tools need to be stated in the form of instructional objectives which reflect the desired outcomes of a course;

b) assessment tools need to possess practical utility, reliability and validity;

c) assessors need to be trained in the use of assessment tools.

Teachers need to select assessment tools which match exactly the learning outcomes that education is intended to promote. , If no such instrument exists, then teachers should develop one. It is important to stress that the instructional objectives should be designed before the assessment tool is selected. In this way, teachers are likely to avoid the inclusion of assessment items that are inappropriate for the outcomes which they desire to measure or assess. This issue is particularly important to nurses' clinical ability, because teachers should not predict clinical skills on the basis of test forms that do not reflect the intended outcomes of teaching-learning situations. In other words, tools should permit observation of the types of performance that the student should demonstrate at the end of the learning experience.

No matter how carefully instructional objectives are selected, there are likely to be unanticipated effects of education. For example, as a result of empathy education, some subjects in this study claimed to be more sensitive to the limits of information. Thus, although instructional objectives provide a useful guide for teaching and assessment, teachers need to be flexible enough to allow for unplanned outcomes. This means that assessment of learning should not depend on formal assessment tools alone. Teachers need to recognise the value of informal observations and judgments as a method of assessment.

There is a need for nurse educators to pay attention to the characteristics of assessment tools because these instruments might be used to predict success or failure in future learning or occupations. Important characteristics of assessment tools are the extent to which they possess practical utility, reliability and validity.

All intended users of assessment tools should be provided with training in their use. This argument is supported by the initial investigation of inter-rater reliability during the present study. This is a concern which needs to be addressed, because failure to train raters is likely to result in unreliable assessments.

The desirability of the above educational design is suggested by the findings of this study. While it is possible that some educators may claim that they are doing it already, a review of the literature reveals no evidence that all of the proposals are being addressed within a single programme. The major barriers to implementation include the low level of the investigation of assessment tools and the tendency of nurse educators to retreat from clinical practice.

The assumption that nurse education needs to invest more time in investigating assessment strategies is suggested by experience of the UK and USA systems, and a review of the literature (e.g. Ashworth and Morrison, 1991; Hepworth, 1991; Coates and Chambers, 1992). The need for more reliable and valid instruments is now attracting interest within nursing, suggesting that this problem can be resolved, providing that teachers have suitable skills and time to investigate assessment tools.

The need for nurse educators to provide direction with clinical nursing has been proposed by numerous writers (e.g. Mauksh, 1980; Reynolds, 1982; Chambers, 1984). A possible explanation for teachers' tendency to withdraw from any involvement with clinical practice is that the perceived needs of the educational institution acts as a barrier to teachers becoming involved with clinical work. Administration and

College-based teaching takes priority over clinical work. It is mandatory, and non-negotiable. Generally speaking, those who are provided with status and financial reward are teachers who have moved further away from clinical practice. In order to reverse this trend, it is necessary to reconsider the reward system. Arguably, the ability to direct clinical practice should be rewarded more highly than administration or classroom teaching.

6.1.1 *The need for nurse educators to remove barriers to clinical empathic behaviour*

Earlier in this Chapter, it was suggested that nurse educators need to ensure that the clinical practice of theory studied in college needs to be guaranteed. This point is critical because the outcomes of this study reveal that barriers to clinical empathy exist in clinical areas (see appendix 9). This suggests that the offer of empathy is not necessarily viewed within the nursing profession as a crucial clinical skill. This conclusion is supported by the findings of earlier studies which reported that nurses do not normally address the specific concerns of clients by showing an understanding of the context and affective dimensions of the client's message (e.g. Haggerty, 1985; McKay et al., 1990). The present study indicates that this may still be happening in many clinical environments. This conclusion is suggested by the reports of lack of time for one-to-one relationships and the fact that some nurses avoided anticipated barriers to clinical work by doing it in their own time.

The situation seems paradoxical in view of the motivation to improve interpersonal skills, expressed by subjects in this study. The explanation may be that while nurses may be interested in the interpersonal aspects of nursing, the reality of the workplace seems to reduce the opportunity to practise these skills. La Monica (1983) suggests that this is due to nurses being unclear about role expectations in terms of their relationships with clients. This possibility is indicated by some subjects' uncertainty about what empathy meant prior to their empathy course. Similarly, George and Larson (1988) suggested that beliefs about the nurse-client relationship range from the mainly social content to the purposeful and therapeutic encounter.

Irrespective of the explanation, this study does reveal a need for teachers to support their students' efforts to practise empathy. This is indicated by the reported feelings of inexperience and anxiety during the fifth clinical interview (Appendix 9, Table 50). While this might indicate realism, it is likely also to be associated with a belief that they should have been doing something else. An important finding was that an antidote to barriers to clinical empathy was the supervisory relationship and the discovery potential of clinical work.

6.1.2 *The responsibility of nurse educators to exhibit empathic behaviour themselves towards students*

A major conclusion, suggested by the outcomes of this study, is that nurse educators need to show empathy towards their students. This is suggested by the numerous references by nurses to experiences that are dependent on empathy. These include: an open, two-way, non-defensive supervisory relationship, direction with clinical work and encouragement to reflect on practice.

It is likely that an empathic supervisor would provide a role model to imitate. The need for this is suggested by the fact that most subjects (prior to empathy education) expressed the view that they could learn how to offer empathy via relationships with other persons. Additionally, in view of the reports of barriers to clinical empathy, there is a need for educators to understand the meaning of their students' experiences, in order to offer interventions that are likely to resolve the problems experienced by students.

6.1.3 *Summary of implications*

In this section, it has been shown that:

a)   the aims of nurse education ought to be concerned with the facilitation of clinical skills, as well as acquiring new knowledge;

b)   there is a need to consider how learning is best organised in order to achieve the aims of education;

c)   in order to facilitate clinical skills teachers need to ensure that their students are able to practise;

d)   teachers need to possess clinical skills and an ability to assist their students to apply their knowledge to clinical work;

e)   there is a need to develop assessment tools which measure the desired outcomes of education, reliably;

f)   if educators offer an empathy course which requires students to offer empathy in clinical environments, they have a responsibility to ensure that their students are able to overcome barriers to clinical empathy;

g)   in order to understand the needs of their students, nurse educators need to display empathy.

The need for this educational design, particularly in relation to clinically focussed empathy education, is suggested by the aims of the health service. The relevance of the findings from this study to the health service are discussed in the next section.

6.2   Implications for the health service

The relevance of the research and developmental findings to the goals of the health service are suggested by the Patients' Charter. For example, the NHS (Scotland) Patients' Charter emphasises that clinicians need to collaborate with users of health services in the prioritising of clinical needs and the setting of treatment goals. The NHS (Scotland) Charter (1992) sets the following standards for health care. Clients should:

a)   share in the responsibility for their own health;

b)   tell professionals what they want;

c)   be entitled to be treated as a person, not a case.

From April, 1992, all hospitals and other health-care providers were required to achieve those outcomes, and to involve clients in their care. As a consequence, the aims of the government charter are reflected in numerous Charters that have been produced by Health Boards, Community Health Councils and NHS Trusts in the UK (e.g. Highland Community Trust - Mental Health Division, 1992; The Association of Community Health Councils for England and Wales, 1992; Highland Health Board, 1994). While the aims of the Patients' Charter seem desirable, it is difficult to understand how they might be achieved unless professionals are able to offer an empathised awareness of the client's expectations and needs. This point is emphasised by Hogg (1994) who pointed out that users, such as women with HIV, or those with the experience of living in pain, have different expectations and needs of the health service from professionals.

The difficulty of understanding the expectations and needs of these clients is indicated by the pre-course levels of empathy reported in this study. Pre-education levels of empathy indicated that nurses entering education possessed levels of empathy that were likely to be too low for understanding the concerns of clients. This conclusion is not only based on the mean score of 29.5 for the test but indicated by the low scores for individual items on the empathy scale which are hypothesised to be critical for investigating the concerns and preferences of clients (items 7 and 9).

It is unlikely that the nurses involved could have assisted clients in this way prior to education when they were obtaining scores of less than two points on several scale items which are critical to assisting a person to investigate experiences. Scores of less than two points indicate a tendency to investigate a client's feelings, perceptions, and goals infrequently. It means that the group were likely to utilise less than twenty five percent of the opportunities to use the following items:

Item 1 : Attempts to explore and clarify feelings.
Item 3 : Responds to feelings.
Item 5 : Explores personal meaning of feelings.
Item 7 : Responds to feeling and meaning.
Item 9 : Provides the client with direction.

In the case of items 7 and 9 the group means were less than one point on the scale. This indicates a tendency to use the approach almost never or never. Because behaviours such as exploring personal meaning of feelings seem so basic to investigating the client's world, nurses could be considered to be low in empathy at that point.

This conclusion is reinforced by the discovery that nurses appeared unwilling to listen to their clients. On two items which are critical to listening, a group mean of less than three points was obtained. These items were:

Item 2 : Leads, directs and diverts.
Item 4 : Ignores verbal and non-verbal behaviour.

An item score of less than three points for negative items indicates that more than fifty percent of responses to clients involved diverting them from concerns and failing to listen to expressed feelings. This tendency, when transmitted to the client, is likely to prevent the client being open, as Mitchell and Berenson (1970) and Valenti (1986) suggest.

The low baseline measures of empathy for the experimental group were similar to those obtained for the control group. Therefore the finding from this study is similar to numerous reports of professionals' inability to provide empathy at a facilitative level (Gagan, 1983; Hughes et al., 1990; Wheeler and Barrett, 1994). Consequently, the outcome of the investigation of pre-course empathy suggests that there remains a need for registered nurses to continue to be provided with empathy education. While it is possible that the problem of low-empathy nursing has been reduced as a consequence of initiatives from nurse education, a review of the recent literature does not provide any evidence of this (see Morrison and Burnard, 1991; Jones, 1995). The low baseline measures of empathy found in this study suggest that it is unlikely that nurse education has resolved the problem of reducing the theory-practice dichotomy that was referred to in Chapter 2. Therefore it seems logical to suggest that at worst, nurse education continues to have a problem in teaching empathy and, at best, subjects in this study had a great deal to learn about empathy prior to education. This suggests that the aims of understanding what the client wants, and the involvement of the client in the setting of treatment outcomes, would be difficult to achieve.

In spite of the fact that nurses on the empathy course achieved gains on pre-course measures of empathy, a concern is that clinical areas presented barriers to the use of empathy in practice. One barrier was the unsympathetic views of colleagues. This finding contrasts with the finding, pre-course, that most nurses wanted to improve their interpersonal skills. A possible explanation for the negative attitude of some colleagues is that staffing levels, workload, rapid discharge and a lack of understanding of the therapeutic potential of empathy, prevents empathy from being regarded as a situational norm (Hughes and Carver, 1990).

Anxiety about peer attitudes to talking one-to-one with the client might decrease if offering empathy to clients was a clear expectation of the workplace. In order to achieve that situation, those in authority (managers) need to model empathy and encourage its use. Such encouragement should include the provision of staffing levels which allow time for prolonged one-to-one relationships and investigation of the effect of rapid discharge from hospital on the opportunity of nurses to know their clients. Additionally, those who purchase education for nurses need to consider the evidence that the empathy course purchased actually enables nurses to learn how to offer empathy in the clinical situation.

The measures suggested here seem necessary in view of the finding that nurses in this study were unable to score highly on the empathy scale item which related to helping the clients to discover their preferred ways of dealing with threats to their health. While nurses made gains on all items on the empathy scale, the ability to help the client to consider options, was the most difficult to learn (item 9).

The item gains for item 5 (+41.6%) and item 7 (+46.6%) indicate that the experimental group were more competent than the control group, in assisting clients to explore circumstances which related to feelings, and demonstrating commitment to the client. However, the extent to which clients were enabled to develop new competencies is open to speculation. At best, the outcome suggests that subjects were attempting to use counselling for the purpose of helping clients to learn something worthwhile by examining experiences. This requires a cognitive effort on the part of subjects which entails purposeful goal directed thinking (Le Fevre, 1995).

While a review of experiences can lead to new insights on the part of the client, this might not be sufficient to change behaviour. Altering health-threatening responses to stressors is likely to be dependent on the nurse's ability to assist clients to select a new and more adaptive coping response. The item on the empathy scale which is focused most directly on assisting the client to select a new coping strategy recorded the lowest percentage gain during training. This item was:

Item 9 : Provides the client with direction.

Why this item was the most resistant to education is of considerable interest to nurse educators. A possible explanation is that this skill was found to be almost non-existent in the sample during baseline measures of empathy. This suggests two things: i) that it is a response which is alien to the nursing culture, and ii) registered nurses have a considerable amount to learn about this therapeutic response. These assumptions are supported by studies reporting a failure by nurses to assist clients to focus on areas of concern (Cormack, 1976 Melia, 1981; Maguire, 1985).

While the aims of the empathy course are not being equated with the goals of counselling training provided by Carkhuff and Truax (1965), the ability to assist the client to identify preferred ways of dealing with illness, and preferred treatment outcomes, is compatible with the aims of the Patients' Charter. The barriers to clinical empathy reported in this study suggest that nurses' difficulty in achieving those aims, should not be unexpected. Nurses need uninterrupted time in order to listen to their clients and hear what they want to happen. For that reason there is a need to address the barriers to clinical empathy. Otherwise, the aims expressed in patients' charters are likely to remain unfulfilled. The issues discussed in this section, when considered with the findings from this study, indicate implications for future research.

6.3   Implications for future research

An extension of this study is suggested. An investigation of the impact of clinical specialties may provide further understanding of the extent to which differing social and organisational contexts influence empathy. Furthermore, because the majority of subjects in this study were female (n = 27), an investigation of the influence of gender role might provide further understanding on the variables which impact upon empathy. This suggestion relates to Beutler et al., (1996) view that client-helper match influences outcomes.

There is a need to investigate the stability of empathy. The outcome may result in a change of attitude among nurse educators towards evaluation of students' clinical performance. Isolated measures of empathy may not tell us very much about an individual's capacity to empathise over time. Empathy may be like blood pressure: it may fluctuate in response to environmental variables such as mood, time and interruptions.

The questions which need to be asked are: "Does empathy markedly fluctuate over time from situation to situation?" and, "Do nurses who do not consistently display high levels of empathy towards associates, consistently display high levels of empathy towards clients?" One way of investigating those questions may be to observe whether clients being seen by the same nurse received similar levels of empathy over a prolonged period of time, and to compare these levels with levels of empathy received by associates over the same time period.

There is also a need to conduct longitudinal post-course measures of empathy. While there are practical limits to the extent to which the investigation of training gains may be delayed, it would be useful to extend this investigation beyond the 3-6 months timespan of this study. This would provide insights into the extent to which training gains are sustained. This would enable educators to understand more about the longer-term efficacy of empathy education, and learn more about variables that may erode or sustain empathy in the workplace.

Remaining tasks for educational research include the need to establish the extent to which workshop learning can be replicated in clinical practice or whether regular clinical supervision or combinations of both are superior in respect of promoting and maintaining nurses' empathy. This may have the effect of making nurse educators more interested in what happens in clinical environments. While there is a great deal of interest among nurse educators in various forms of workshop education, the impact of this on clinical practice is poorly understood.

There is a need for educators to address the realities of clinical practice. In order to do this, studies are needed which investigate the expressed concerns of clients during brief contacts with nurses. These data may enable educators to construct a learning process which would enable nurses to utilise brief contacts more effectively. A teaching programme which enables nurses to be therapeutic during all types of contacts with clients, formal and informal, is likely to be more credible within the nurse culture.

A possible limitation of the empathy scale is that it focuses almost exclusively on verbal behaviour. Non-verbal aspects of communication such as eye contact, body posture and touch, were deliberately excluded because they could not be assessed from audiotapes. However, Kunst-Wilson et al. (1981) point out that non-verbal behaviour is of considerable importance when understanding and feelings are communicated to the client. For this reason it would be useful to study the relationship between subjects' ratings on the empathy scale with assessments of their non-verbal behaviour. Client reports, videotaped records, or non participant observations of non-verbal behaviour could be utilised. These data would yield further insights into the construct validity of the empathy scale, because low-empathy persons are said to exhibit avoidance of eye contact, extensive head-nodding and frequent gesturing, while high-empathy persons exhibit a steady gaze, moderate head-nodding, and limited gesturing (Lyons-Halaris, 1979). The study proposed here would be relevant to the construct validity of the empathy scale because it would be a way of identifying persons in whom a quality or predisposition is likely to occur (Cronbach and Meehl, 1955).

A further method of investigating the construct validity of the empathy scale would be to conduct experimental studies designed to investigate the influence of empathic nurses on health outcomes for clients. Nurses in this study claimed that they were helping clients with a variety of problems. Those included anxiety, guilt, adjusting to loss and change, low self-esteem, and pain. Client outcome studies of such problems would provide an opportunity to investigate the relationship between the scale and the hypothesised relationship between empathy and favourable health outcomes for clients.

While the hypothesised relationship between empathy and helping has been extensively investigated, most of the research has involved non-nursing contexts. Where research has been conducted with nurses, the study designs have not been experimental and usually have not focused on specific health outcomes. If a correlation can be demonstrated between nurses' empathy and specific health outcomes for clients, those who manage clinical nursing may be motivated to try to improve the low levels of empathy existing within nursing at the present time.

6.4   Summary of opportunities for nurse education

In this chapter, it has been shown that the aims of nurse education ought to be concerned with what students can do clinically, in order to help clients, as well as what students know. In order to achieve that aim it has been suggested that teachers ought to be aware of the limitations to learning in clinical environments, and support their students' efforts to apply their theory of helping, such as empathy, in the reality of the real training situation. This suggests that teachers need to possess a range of abilities, including an empathised awareness of barriers which inhibit students' ability to offer empathy in clinical environments. It is necessary also that teachers possess reliable and valid measures of the desired outcomes of education.

The findings of this study suggest that the aims of the health service are unlikely to be met by the low levels of empathy that continue to exist in clinical nursing. However, the outcome of this study encourages the view that the new empathy course can resolve this problem, provided that teachers and managers work together in order to resolve the barriers that affect nurses' ability to offer clinical empathy. Unless this occurs, it is unlikely that nurses and other professionals will be able to achieve a collaborative relationship with clients which aims to prioritise clinical needs and set treatment goals.

This study indicates numerous directions for future research. These include the extent to which gender and specific clinical areas affect nurses' ability to offer empathy. It is necessary also to investigate further the extent to which the learning outcomes of empathy education are sustained and whether empathy is situational related.

While this study suggests that the nature of the supervisory relationship and the discovery potential of experiential clinical work are critical components of empathy education, the extent to which workshop learning can be replicated in clinical practice is unknown. The contribution of clinical workshops merits further investigation.

There is a need also for researchers to investigate how best to help nurses to empathise during brief contacts with clients. These interactions represent the reality of most nurse-client interactions. Such a study would enable nurse educators to understand the clinical usefulness of empathy in nursing contexts, and how to enable nurses to utilise these contacts for the benefit of their clients.

Finally, there is a need to investigate further the construct validity of the new empathy scale. Such an investigation could involve a study of the relationship between nurses' scores on the empathy scale and their non-verbal behaviour. Crucially, it is also important to investigate the relationship between subjects' scores on the scale and measurable benefits for clients.

Bibliography

Alexander, M (1983) *Learning to Nurse: Integrating Theory and Practice. Ph.D.* Thesis, University of Edinburgh.

Allcock, N (1992) Teaching the skills of communication through the use of an experiential workshop. *Nurse Education Today.* V12, pp 287-292.

Altmann, H (1983) *Effects of Empathy, Warmth and Genuineness in the Initial Counselling Interview. Counsellor Education and Supervision.* V12, pp 225-228.

Altschul, A (1972) *Patient-Nurse Interaction: A Study of Interaction Patterns in Acute Psychiatric Wards.* Churchill Livingstone, Edinburgh.

Anderson, H and Gerrard, B (1984) *A Comprehensive Interpersonal Skills Programme for Nurses, Journal of Nursing Education.* V23 (8), pp 353 355.

Anthony, W (1971) *A Methodological Investigation of the Minimally Facilitative Level of Interpersonal Functioning. Journal of Clinical Psychology.* V27, pp 156-157.

Ashworth, P (1980) *Care of Communicate: An Investigation into Problems of Communication Between Patients and Nurses in Intensive Therapy Unit.* RCN, London.

Ashworth, P and Morrison, P (1991) Problems of competence based nurse education. *Nurse Education Today.* V11, pp 256 - 260.

Aspey, D (1965) *A Study of Three Facilitative Conditions and their Relationship to the Achievement of Third Grade Students.* Ph.D. Thesis, University of Kentucky.

Aspey, D (1975) Empathy: Lets get the hell on with it. *The Counselling Psychologist.* V5, pp 10-14.

Aspey, D and Roebuck, F (1975) A discussion of the relationship between selected student behaviour and the teacher's use of interchangeable responses. *Human Education.* V1(3), pp 3-10.

Auger, J and Dee, V (1982) A Patient Classification System based on the Behavioural System of Nursing. *Journal of Nursing Administration.* (April), pp 38-48.

Ausubel, D (1963) *The Psychology of Meaningful Verbal Learning.* Grune and Stratton, NY.

Bachrach, H; Luborsky, L; Mechanick, P (1974) The Correspondence Between Judgments of Empathy from Brief Samples of Psychotherapy; Supervisors Judgments and Sensitivity Tests. *British Journal of Medical Psychology,* V47, pp 337-340.

Bachrach, H (1976) Empathy: We Know What We Mean, But What Do We Measure? *Archives of General Psychiatry.* pp 404-407.

Baillie, L (1995) Empathy in the nurse-patient relationship. *Nursing Standard.* V9, pp 29-30.

Bandura, A (1977) *Social Learning Theory.* Prentice Hall, New Jersey.

Barker, P (1994) Locus of control in women with a diagnosis of manic-depressive psychosis. *Journal of Psychiatric and Mental Health Nursing.* V1, pp 9-14.

Barret-Lennard, G (1981) The empathy cycle: refinement of a nuclear concept. *Journal of Counselling Psychology.* V28, pp 91 -100.

Bendall, R (1976) Learning for reality. *Journal of Advanced Nursing.* V41, pp 3-9.

Bennett, J (1995) "Methodological notes on empathy" Further considerations. *Advanced Nursing Science.* V18, pp 36-50.

Bergin, A; Garfield, S (1971*) Handbook of Psychotherapy and Behaviour Change.* John Wiley and Sons, NY.

Beutler, L; Heidi, A; Williams, R (1996) Research Applications of Prescriptive Therapy. In Dryden, W (Ed*). Research in Counselling and Psychotherapy: Practical applications.* Sage Publications, London.

Bishop, V (1994) Clinical supervision for an accountable profession. *Nursing Times.* V90, pp 35-37.

Bloom, J (1982) Social Support Accommodation to Stress and Adjustment to Breast Cancer. *Social Science and Medicine.* V16, pp 1329-38.

Boydell, T (1976) *Experiential Learning.* Manchester Monograph No. 5, University of Manchester.

Bregg, E (1958) How can we help students learn? *The American Journal of Nursing.* V58 (8) pp 1120-1122.

Briggs, E (1982) Interpersonal Skills: Training for Nurses During Introductory Course. *Nurse Education Today.* V2, pp 22-24.

Brennan, A (1993) Perceptorship: is it a workable concept? *Nursing Standard.* V7, pp 34-36.

Brockhaus, J (1971) The Effect of a Training Programme on the Empathic Ability of Psychiatric Aides. Us Department of Health, Education and Welfare (Project No. OFO96).

Brown, G; Harris, T (1978) *The Social Origins of Depression.* Tavistock, London.

Burnard, P (1992 a) Defining experiential learning: nurse tutors' perceptions. *Nurse Education Today,* V1, pp 29-36.

Burnard, P (1992 b) Student nurses' perceptions of experiential learning. *Nurse Education Today.* V12, pp 163-173.

Burnard, P; Chapman, C (1990) *Nurse Education: The Way Forward.* Scutari Press, London.

Caracena, P; Vicory, J (1969) Correlates of Phenomenological and Judged Empathy. *Journal of Counselling Psychology.* V 16, pp 510-515.

Carkuff, R; Truax, C (1965) Training in Counselling and Psychotherapy: an evaluation of an integrated didactic and experiential approach. *Journal of Counselling Psychology.* V29, pp 333-336.

Carkuff, R; Truax, C (1967) *Towards Effective Counselling and Psychotherapy.* Aldine-Atherton, NY.

Carkuff, R; Berenson, B (1967) *Beyond Counselling and Therapy.* Holt, NY.

Carkuff, R (1976) *Helping and Human Relations.* Holt, NY.

Carver, E; Hughes, J (1990) The Significance of Empathy. In MacKay, R; Hughes, J and Carver, E (Eds.) *Empathy in the Helping Relationship.* Springer Publishing Co, NY.

Chambers, M (1990) Psychiatric and mental health nursing: learning in the clinical environment. In Reynolds, W; Cormack, D (Eds.) *Psychiatric and Mental Health Nursing Theory and Practice.* Chapman and Hall, London.

Chambers, M (1994) *Learning Psychiatric Nursing Skills: The Contribution of the Ward Environment.* Ph.D. Thesis, University of Ulster.

Chapman, C (1983) The paradox of nursing. *Journal of Advanced Nursing.* V 8, pp 269-272.

Christiansen, C (1977) Measuring Empathy in Occupational Therapy Students. *Journal of Occupational Therapy.* V31, pp 19-22.

Clinton, M (1985) Training Psychiatric Nurses: Why Theory Into Practice Won't Go. In Altschul, A (Ed) *Psychiatric Nursing.* Churchill Livingstone, Edinburgh.

Coates, V; Chambers, M (1992) Evaluation of tools to assess clinical competence. *Nurse Education Today.* V12, pp 122-128.

Coffman, S (1981) Empathy as a relevant instructor variable in the experiential classroom. *Group and Organisational Studies.* V6, pp 114-120.

Collins, M (1983) *Communication in Health Care.* Mosby, St Louis, MO.

Cook, L (1993) Cited in Hogg, A (1994) *Working with users: Beyond the patients' charter.* Health Rights Ltd, Brixton, London.

Costello, J (1989) Learning from each other: peer teaching and learning in student nurse training. *Nurse Education Today.* V9, pp 203-206.

Cormack, D (1976) *A Descriptive Study of the work of The Charge Nurse in Acute Admission Units of Psychiatric Hospitals.* M.Phil Thesis, Dundee College of Technology.

Cormack, D (1981) Making Use of Unsolicited Research data. *Journal of Advanced Nursing.* V6, pp 41-49.

Cormack, D (1983) *Psychiatric Nursing Described.* Churchill Livingstone, Edinburgh.

Cormack, D (1985) The Myths and Realities of Interpersonal Skills Use in Nursing. In Kagan, C(Ed.) *Interpersonal Skills in Nursing: Research and Application.* Croom Helm: London.

Cronbach, L; Meehl, F (1955) Construct Validity in Psychological Tests. *Psychological Bulletin,* V52, pp 281- 302.

Davis, M (1983) The effects of dispositional empathy on emotional reactions and helping: A multidimensional approach. *Journal of Personality.* V51, pp 167-184.

Dawson, C (1985) Hypertension, perceived clinician empathy and patient self-disclosure. *Research in Nursing and Health.* V8 pp 191-198.

Denton, S; Baum, M (1982) Can we predict which women will fail to cope with mastectomy? In Margalese, R (Ed) *Breast Cancer.* Churchill Livingstone, Edinburgh.

Detterman, D; Sternberg, R (1982) *How and by How Much can Intelligence be Increased?* Norwood, NJ, Ablex.

Dietrich, G (1978) Teaching Psychiatric Nursing in the Classroom. *Journal of Advanced Nursing.* V 3, pp 525-534.

Disiker, R; Michiellute, A (1981) An Analysis of Empathy in Medical Students Before and Following Clinical Experience. *Journal of Medical Education.* V56, pp 1004 - 1010.

Dittes, J (1957) Galvanic skin response as a measure of patients' reaction to therapist permissiveness. *Journal of Abnormal Psychology.* V18, pp 191-196.

Dowie, S: Park, C (1988) Relating nursing theory to students' life experiences. *Nurse Education Today.* V8, pp 191-196.

Duff, R; Hollinwood, A (1968) *Sickness and Society.* Harper Row, NY.

Duncan, M; Biddle, B (1974) *The Study of Teaching.* Holt-Reinhart, Winston.

Durheim, R (1993) Student nurses' perception of the clinical midwifery experiences as a learning environment. *Cairatonis.* V16, pp 1-5.

Egan, G (1986) *The Skilled Helper.* Brooks-Cole Publishing Co. Monterey, California.

Ellis, F; Watson, C (1985) *Learning Through the Patient.* Nursing Times. V81, pp 52-54.

Faulkner, A (1985) Organisational Context of Interpersonal Skills in Nursing. In Kagan, C (Ed) *Interpersonal Skills in Nursing: Research and Applications.* Croom Helm: London.

Feital, B (1968) *Feeling Understood as a Variety of Therapist Activities.* Ph.D. Thesis, Teachers' College, Columbia University.

Fielding, R; Llewelyn, S (1987) Communication training in nursing may damage your health and enthusiasm: some warning. *Journal of Advanced Nursing.* V12, pp 281 - 290.

Fox, F (1983) *Fundamentals of Research in Nursing* (4th Ed) Appleton - Century - Crofts, Connecticut.

Friehofer, P; Felton, G (1976) Nursing Behaviours in Bereavement: An Exploratory Study. *Nursing Research.* V25, pp 332-337.

Gagan, J (1983) Methodological Notes on Empathy. *Advances in Nursing Science.* pp 65-72.

Gazda, G: Asbury, F; Balzer, F; Childers, W; Walters, R (1984) *Human Relations Development: A manual for Educators* (3rd Ed). Albyn and Bacon Inc., Boston.

Gazda, G; Childers, W; Walters, R (1977) *Interpersonal Communication: a handbook for health professionals.* Aspen Publishers: Rockville, MD.

Gazda, G; Walters, R; Childers, W (1975) *Human Relations Development: A Manual for Health Sciences.* Albyn and Bacon: Boston, MA.

George, T; Larsen, J (1988) The culture of nursing. In Baumgurt, J; Larsen, J (Eds.) *Canadian Nursing faces the Future* (pp 63-74). C.V. Mosby Co, Toronto.

Gerrard, B (1978) *The Construction and Validation of a Behavioural Test for Interpersonal Skills for Health Professionals.* Unpublished manuscript. Department of medicine: McMaster University.

Gladstein, G (1977) Empathy and counselling outcome: an empirical and conceptual review. *The Counselling Psychologist.* V6, pp 70-79.

Gordon, M (1987) *Nursing Diagnosis: Process and Allocation.* McGraw-Hill: NY.

Gow, K (1982) *How Nurses Emotions Affect Patient Care.* Springer Publishing Co., NY.

Graham, M (1993) Parental sensitivity to infant cues similarities and differences between mothers and fathers. *Journal of Paediatric Nursing.* V8, pp 376 - 384.

Grief, E; Hogan, R (1973) The Theory and Measurement of Empathy. *Journal of Counselling Psychology.* V2, pp 280-284.

Griffin, A (1983) A philosophical analysis of caring in nursing. *Journal of Advanced Nursing.* V8, pp 289-295.

Guttman, M; Haase, R (1972) Generalisation of microcounselling skills from training period to actual counselling setting. *Counsellor Education and Supervision.* V12(2), pp 99-108.

Haggerty, L (1985) A theoretical model for developing students' communication skills. *Journal of Nursing Education.* V24, pp296 -298.

Haines, J (1987) Aids: New considerations in caring. *The Canadian Nurse.* V77, pp 11-12.

Hart, J (1960) *A Replication of the Halkides Study.* Unpublished Manuscript, University of Wisconsin.

Heine, R (1950) *A Comparison of Patients' reports on Psychotherapeutic Experience with psychoanalytic, Nondirective and Adlerian Therapists.* Doctoral dissertation, University of Chicago.

Hepworth, S (1991) The assessment of student nurses. *Nurse Education Today.* V11, pp 46-52.

Highland Community Trust: Mental health division (1992) *The Patients' Charter*, Brochure.

Highland Health Board (1994) *A Health Charter for the People of the Highlands.* Brochure.

Hills, M; Knowles, D (1983) Nurses levels of empathy and respect in simulated interactions with patients. *International Journal of Nursing Studies.* V20, pp 83-87.

Hogg, A (1994) *Working with Users: Beyond the patients' charter.* Health Rights Ltd. Brixton, London.

Howard, J (1975) Humanisation, dehumanisation of health care. In Howard, J; Strauss, A (Eds.) *Humanising Health Care.* John Wiley, NY.

Howell, (1989) *Fundamental statistics for the behavioural sciences* (2nd ed.). PWS Kent: Boston.

Hughes, J: Carver, E; MacKay, R (1990) Learning to Use Empathy. In MacKay, R; Hughes, J; Carver, E (Eds.) *Empathy in the Helping Relationship.* Springer Publishing Co., NY.

Hughes, R; Huckill, H (1982) *Participant Characteristics: Change and Outcome in Preservice Clinical Teachers' Education.* Report No. 9020: Research and Development Centre for Teacher Education. University of Texas, Austin.

Hung, J; Rosenthal, T (1978) Therapeutic Playback: A Critical review. *Advances in Behaviour Research and Therapy.* V1, pp 103-135.

Jaffray, L (1995) Patient care: from nurse to patient and back again. *Nursing Standard.* V9, pp 50-51.

Johnstone, J; Cheek, J; Smither, R (1983) The Structure of empathy. *Journal of Personality and Social Psychology.* V43, pp 1299-1312.

Jones, A (1995) The organisational influence on counselling relationships in a general hospital setting. *Journal of Psychiatric and Mental Health Nursing.* V2, pp 83-89.

Juneck, W; Burra, P; Leshner, P (1979) Teaching Interviewing Skills by Encountering Patients. *Journal of Medical Education.* V54, pp 402-407.

Kagan, N (1973) *Influencing Human Interaction - Eleven years of IPR.* Paper presented at the American Educational Research Association. Annual Convention. New Orleans.

Kagan, N (1990) IPR - A Validated Model for the 1990's and Beyond. *The Counselling Psychologist.* Vol. 18, pp 436-440.

Kalish, B (1971) An Experiment in the Development of Empathy in Nursing Students. *Nursing Research.* V20, pp 202-211.

Kalish, B (1973) What is Empathy? *American Journal of Nursing.* V73, pp 1548-1552.

Kalkman, M (1967) *Psychiatric Nursing.* McGraw-Hill, NY.

Keatochvii, D (1967). The differential effects of absolute level and direction of growth in counsellor functioning, upon clients' functioning. *Journal of Clinical psychologist.* V23, pp 216-217.

Keeton, M et al. (1988) *Experiential Learning.* Jossey Bass, San Francisco.

Kendall, P; Wilcox, L (1980) Cognitive-Behavioural Treatment for Impulsivity: Concrete VS Conceptual Training in Non Self-controlled Problem Children. *Journal of Consulting and Clinical Psychology.* V48, pp 80-91.

Kershmer, J; La Monica, E (1976) *Effectiveness of Nursing Curricula on Behavioural Empathy.* Unpublished research report. University of Massachusetts.

Kickbush, I; Hatch, S (1983) An Orientation of Health Care. In Hatch, S & Kickbush, I (Eds.) *Self-help and Health in Europe: New Approaches in Health Care*. World Health Organisation, Copenhagen.

Kielser, D; Mathieu, P; Klein, M (1967) Summary of the Issues and Conclusions. In Rogers, C; Kiesler, D; Gendlin, A; Truax, C(Eds.). *The Therapeutic Relationship and its Impact: A Study of Psychotherapy with Schizophrenics*. Madison, University of Wisconsin Press.

Kirk, W (1979) *The Effect of Interpersonal Process Recall Method Training, and Interpersonal Communication Training on the Empathic Behaviour of Psychiatric Nursing Personnel*. Doctoral Thesis: University of Kansas.

Knowles, M (1980) The modern practice of adult education. Cited in Jarvis, P; Gibson, S(Eds.) *The Teacher Practitioner in Nursing, Midwifery and Health Visiting*. Croom Helm, London.

Kolb, D (1984) *Learning Style Inventory: Technical Manual*. McBer, Boston.

Kreigh, H; Perko, J (1979) *Psychiatric and Mental Health Nursing: A Commitment to Care and Concern*. Reston Publishing Co., Virginia

Kunst-Wilson, W; Carpenteri, L; Poser, A; Venohr, I; Kushner, K (1981) Empathic Perceptions of Nursing Students: Self-Reported and Actual Ability. *Research in Nursing and Health*. V4, pp 283-293.

La Fevere, R (1995) *Critical Thinking in Nursing: A Practical Approach*. W B Saunders, Philadelphia.

La Monica, E (1979) Empathy in nursing practice. *Issues in Mental Health Nursing*. V2, pp 2 -13.

La Monica, E (1981) Construct Validity of an Empathy Instrument. *Research in Nursing and Health*. V4, pp 389-400.

La Monica, E (1983) Empathy can be learned. *Nurse Educator*. pp 19-23.

La Monica, E; Carew, D; Winder, A; Haase, A; Blanchard, K (1976) Empathy Training as the Major Thust of a Staff Development Programme. *Nursing Research*. V25, pp 447-451.

La Monica, E; Madea, A; Oberst, M (1987) Empathy and nursing care outcomes. *Scholarly Inquiry for Nursing Practice*. V1, pp 197-213.

Lave, J; Wenger, E (1991) *Situated Learning: Legitimate Peripheral Participation*. Cambridge University Press, Cambridge.

Law, E (1978) *Toward the Teaching and measurement of Empathy for Staff Nurses*. Ph.D. Thesis, Brigham Young University, Utah.

Layton, J (1979) The Use of Modelling to Teach Empathy to Nursing Students. *Research in Nursing and Health*. V2, pp 163-176.

Lazarus, R; Folkman, S (1984) *Stress Appraisal and Coping*. Springer Publishing Company, New York.

Lewis, J (1974) Practicum in Attention to Affect: A Course for Beginning Psychotherapists. *Psychiatry*. V37, pp 109-113.

Lyons-Halaris, A (1979) *Relationship of Perceived Empathy to Nurses' Non-Verbal Communication*. Masters Thesis, University of Illinois.

Macilwaine, H (1990) *The Nursing of Female Neurotic Patients in Psychiatric Units of General Hospitals*. Ph.D. Thesis, University of Manchester.

MacKay, R; Hughes, J; Carver, E (1990) *Empathy in the Helping Relationship*. Springer Publishing Co, NY.

MacLeod-Clarke, J (1983) Nurse-Patient Communications: An analysis of conversations from surgical wards. In Wilson-Barnett, J(Ed.) *Nursing Research: Ten Studies in Patient Care*. Wiley, Chichester.

MacLeod-Clarke, J (1985) The Development of Research in Interpersonal Skills in Nursing. In Kagan, C(Ed.) *Interpersonal Skills in Nursing: Research and Applications*. Croom Helm, London.

Maguire, P (1985) Psychological Reactions in Breast Cancer and its Treatment. In Bonnadonna, G(Ed.) *Breast Cancer, Diagnosis and Management*. Wiley , Chichester.

Maguire, P; Van Dam, F (1983) Psychological aspects of breast cancer: Workshop report. *European Journal of Cancer and Clinical Oncology*. V19, pp 1735-1740.

Mariju, J (1988) *Cited in SPSS/PC and Advanced Statistics* (V2.0) SPSS International BU, Chicago.

Marshall, K (1977) Empathy, Genuineness and Regard: Determinant of Successful Therapy With Schizophrenics. *Psychotherapy Theory, Research and Practice*. V14, pp 57-64.

Marshfield, G (1985) Issues Arising from Teaching Interpersonal Skills in General Nurse Training. In Kagan, C(Ed.) *Interpersonal Skills in Nursing: Research and Applications*. Croom Helm, London.

Marson, S (1982) Developing Skills in Communication 1: An Interactive Approach. *Nurse Education Today*. V2, pp 12-14.

Martin, J and Curkhuff, R (1968) Changes in personality and interpersonal functioning of counsellors in training. *Journal of Clinical Psychology*. V24, pp 104-110.

Mauksh, I (1980) Faculty practice: a professional imperative. *Nurse Educator*. V5, pp 7-11.

McGinnis, P (1987) Teaching Nurses to Teach. In Davis, B(Ed.) *Nursing Education: Research and Developments*. Croom Helm: London.

Melia, K (1981) Student Nurses' Construction of Nursing: A Discussion of a Qualitative Method. *Nursing Times*. V77, pp 697 - 699.

Messick, A (1989) Intergroup relations. *Annual review of Psychology*. V40, pp 45-81.

Miller, W; Hedrick, K; Orlofsky, D (1980) *The Helpful Response Questionnaire*. Unpublished paper, University of New Mexico, Albuquerque.

Mintz, J; Luborsky (1971) Dimensions of Psychotherapy: A Factor Analytic Study of Ratings of Psychotherapy Sessions. *Journal of Consulting Clinical Psychology.* V36, pp 106-120.

Mintz, J; Luborsky (1971) Segments versus Whole Sessions: Which is the Better Unit for Psychotherapy Research? *Journal of Abnormal Psychology.* V78, pp 180-191.

Mitchell, K; Berenson, B (1970) Differential use of Confrontation by High and Low Facilitative Therapists. *Journal of Nervous Mental Disorder.* V51, pp 303-309.

Morrison, P; Burnard, P (1991) *Caring and Communicating: The Interpersonal relationship in Nursing.* MacMillan Education, Hampshire.

Morse, J; Anderson, G; Botter, J; Yonge, O; Obrien, B; Solberg, S (1992) Exploring Empathy: A Conceptual Fit for Nursing Practice? *Image: Journal of Nursing Scholarship.* V24, pp 273-280.

Morse, J; Miles, M; Clarke, D; Doberneck, B (1994) Sensing patient needs: exploring concepts of nursing insight and receptivity used in nursing assessment. *Scholarly Inquiry for Nursing Practice.* V8, pp 233-260.

Murphy, J (1971) The Nub of the Learning Process. *American Journal of Nursing.* V7, pp 306-310.

Newall, M (1980) The effect of therapist empathy, normal disclosure, self-disclosure and attraction to the therapist. *From Dissertation Abstracts International,* No 34128.

NHS (Scotland) Patients' Charter (1992) *Frame-Work for Action.* The Scottish Office.

Nicol, E; Withington, D (1981) Recorded Patient-Nurse Interaction: An Advance in Psychiatric Nursing. *Nursing Times,* pp 1351-1352.

Northouse, L (1981) Mastectomy patients and fear of cancer recurrence. *Cancer Nursing.* V4. pp 213-220.

Novak, J (1991) Clarify with Concept Maps. *The Science Teacher.* V7, pp 45-49.

Novak, J; Gowan, D (1986) *Learning How to Learn.* Cambridge University Press, NY.

Nunally, J (1972) *Psychometric Theory.* McGraw-Hill, NY.

Oppenheim, A (1992) *Questionnaire Design. Interviewing and Attitude Measurement.* Pinter Publishing Co., London.

Orlando, I (1972) *The Discipline and Teaching of Nursing Process.* Putman: NY.

O'Toole, A; Welt, S (1994) *Interpersonal Theory in Nursing Practice: Selected Works of Hildagard Peplau.* Springer Publishing Co, NY.

Patterson, C (1974) *Relationship Counselling and Psychotherapy.* Harper and Row: NY.

Peitchinis, J (1972) Therapeutic effectiveness of counselling by nursing personnel. *Nursing Research.* V21 (2), pp 138-148.

Peplau, H (1952) *Interpersonal Relations in Nursing: A Conceptual Frame of Reference for Psychodynamic Nursing.* Putman: NY.

Peplau, H (1957) What is experiential teaching? *American Journal of Nursing.* V57, pp 884-886.

Peplau, H (1984) *Therapeutic Nurse-patient Interactions.* Paper presented at Hamilton Psychiatric Hospital, Hamilton, Ontario.

Peplau, H (1987) Interpersonal Constructs for Nursing Practice. *Nurse Education Today.* V7, pp 201-208.

Peplau, H (1988) *Substance and Scope of Psychiatric Nursing.* Paper presented at the Third Canadian Conference on Psychiatric Nursing, Montreal.

Peplau, H (1990) Interpersonal relations model: theoretical constructs, principles and general applications. In Reynolds, W; Cormack, D (Eds.) *Psychiatric and Mental Health Nursing: Theory and Practice.* Chapman and Hall. London.

Peplau, H (1995) Cited in O'Toole, A; Welt, S(Eds.) *Hidegard, E, Peplau:* Selected Works. Macmillan, NY.

Petit, M (1981) Battered Women: A nearly hidden social problem. In Getty, C; Humphreys, W (Eds.) *Understanding the Family: Stress and Change in American Life.* Appleton-Century-Croft: NY.

Polgar, C; Thompson, S (1988) *Introduction to Research in Health Sciences.* Churchill Livingston, Edinburgh.

Polit, D; Hungler, B (1983) *Nursing Research: Principles and Methods:* Lippincott Co, Philadelphia.

Rappaport, J; Chinsky, J (1972) Accurate Empathy Confusion of a Construct. *Psychological Bulletin.* V77, pp 400-404.

Raudonis, B (1993) The meaning and impact of empathic relationships in hospice nursing. *Cancer Nursing.* V16, pp 304-309.

Reid, B (1993) 'But we are doing it already': Exploring a response to the concept of reflective practice in order to improve its facilitation. *Nurse Education Today.* V15, pp 305-309.

Reynolds, W (1982) Patient-Centred Teaching: A Future Role for the Psychiatric Nurse Teacher? *Journal of Advanced Nursing.* V7, pp 469 - 475.

Reynolds, W (1985) Issues Arising from Teaching Interpersonal Skills in Psychiatric Nursing. In Kagan, C(Ed.) *Interpersonal Skills in Nursing: Research and Applications.* Croom Helm, London.

Reynolds, W (1986) *A Study of Empathy in Student Nurses.* M.Phil Thesis, Dundee College of Technology.

Reynolds, W (1987) Empathy: We know what we mean, but what do we teach? *Nurse Education Today.* V7, pp 265-269.

Reynolds, W (1989) *Professional Studies Module: The empathy course.* Internal Document of the University of Stirling, Highland Campus, Inverness.

Reynolds, W (1990) Teaching psychiatric and mental health nursing: a teaching perspective. In Reynolds, W; Cormack, D (Eds.) *Psychiatric and Mental Health Nursing: Theory and Practice.* Chapman and Hall, London.

Reynolds, W (1994) The influence of clients' perceptions of the helping relationship in the development of an empathy scale. *Journal of Psychiatric and Mental Health Nursing.* V1, pp 23-30.

Reynolds, W; Cormack, D (Eds.) (1990) *Psychiatric and Mental Health Nursing: Theory and Practice.* Chapman and Hall, London.

Reynolds, W; Presly, A (1988) A study of empathy in student nurses. *Nurse Education Today.* V8, pp 123-130.

Ritter, S (Ed.) (1994) *Manual of Clinical Psychiatric Nursing Principles and Procedures.* Chapman and Hall, London.

Rocher, O (1977) The effects of open and closed inquiry modes used by counsellors and physicians in an initial interview on the interviewee perceptions and self disclosures. *Dissertation Abstracts International.* Abstract No. 7458A-7549A.

Rogers, C (1957) The necessary and sufficient conditions of therapeutic personality change. *Journal of Consulting Psychology.* V21, pp 95-103.

Rogers, C (1960) Self-Directed Education: Change In Action. *Epilogue in Freedom to Learn.* Merrill: Columbus, OH.

Rogers, C (1961) *On Becoming a Person.* Houghton Mifflin Boston, MA.

Rogers, C (1967) *The Therapeutic Relationship and Its Impact.* University of Wisconsin Press, Madison, Wisconsin.

Rogers, C (1969) *Freedom to Learn.* Merrill: Columbus, OH.

Rogers, C (1975) Empathic: An unappreciated way of being. *The Counselling Psychologist.* V5, pp 2-10.

Rogers, C (1977) *Carl Rogers on Personal Power.* Delacorte, NY.

Rogers, C (1990) *A Way of Being.* Houghton Mifflin Co: Boston.

Rogers, C; Truax, C (1966) Therapeutic conditions antecedent to change: a theoretical view. In Rogers, C(Ed.) *The Therapeutic Relationship and its Impact: A Study of Psychotherapy with Schizophrenics.* University of Wisconsin Press.

Rogers, I (1986) The effects of undergraduate nursing education on empathy. *Western Journal of Nursing Research.* V8, pp 329-342.

Roper, N; Logan, W and Tierney, A. (1990) *The Elements of Nursing: A Model for Nurses Based on a Model of Living.* Churchill Livingstone, Edinburgh.

Roy, C (1980) *The Roy Adaptation Model.* Prentice Hall, London.

Rytledge, D (1982) Nurses' Knowledge of breast reconstruction: a catalyst for earlier treatment of breast cancer? *Cancer Nursing.* V5, pp 469-474.

Schalk-Thomas, P (1990) Nursing Research: an experiential approach. Mosby, St. Louis.

Schon, D (1987) *Educating the Reflective Practitioner.* Jossey-Bass, San Francisco.

Schwab, J (1962) *The Teaching of Science as Inquiry. In The Teaching of Science.* Cambridge, Massachusetts, Harvard University Press.

Seigal, C (1972) Changes in play therapy behaviours over time, as a function of different levels of therapists offered conditions. *Journal of Clinical Psychology*. V28, p 235.

Shapiro, T (1969) Empathy, Warmth and Genuineness in Psychotherapy. *British Journal of Clinical Psychology*. V38, pp 343-373.

Sloane, J (1993) Offences and defences against patients: A psychoanalytic view of the borderline between empathic failure and malpractice. *Canadian Journal of Psychiatry*. V38, pp 265-273.

Sloane, R; Staples, E (1975) Truax factors, speech characteristics and therapeutic outcome. *Journal of Nervous and Mental Disease*. V163, pp 135-140.

Smith, P (1995) Health and the Curriculum: An eliminative evaluation - Part 2. *Nurse Education Today*. V15 (5), pp 317-322.

Smoyak, S (1990) General systems model: principles and general applications. In Reynolds, W; Cormack, D (Eds.) *Psychiatric and Mental Health Nursing: Theory and Practice*. Chapman and Hall: London.

Squier, R (1990) A Model of Empathic Understanding and Adherence to Treatment Regimes: In Practitioner-Patient Relationships. *Social Science Medicine*. V30, pp 325-339.

Stockhausen, L (1994) The Clinical learning Spiral: A model to develop reflective practitioners. *Nurse Education*. V15, pp 305-309.

Storch, J (1982) *Patients' Rights: Ethical and Legal Issues in Health Care and Nursing*. McGraw-Hill Ryerson, Toronto.

Tait, A (1985) Interpersonal Skill Issues from Mastectomy Nursing Contexts. In Kagan, C (Ed.) *Interpersonal Skills in Nursing: Research and Applications*. Croom Helm, London.

The Association of Community Health Councils for England and Wales (1992) The Patients' Charter. Pamphlet.

Thompson, V; Lakin, M; Johnson, B (1965) Sensitivity Training and Nurse Education. *Nursing Research*. V14, pp 132-137.

Towell, (1975) Understanding Psychiatric Nursing. RCN London.

Treece, E; Treece, J (1982) *Elements of Research in Nursing*. CV Mosby Co, St Louis.

Truax, C (1961) A Scale for the Measurement of Accurate Empathy. *Wisconsin Psychiatric Institute: Discussion Paper 20*. Madison, Wisconsin.

Truax, C (1970) Length of Therapist Response, Accurate Empathy and Patient Improvement. *Journal of Clinical Psychology*. V26, pp 539 -541.

Truax, C; Carkhuff, R (1967) *Toward Effective Counselling and Psychotherapy: Training and Practice*. Aldine, Chicago.

Truax, C; Mitchell, K (1971) Research on certain therapist interpersonal skills in relation to process and outcome. In Bergin, A; Garfield, S (Eds.) *Handbook of psychotherapy: An empirical evaluation*. Wiley, NY.

Valenti, C (1986) Working with physically abused women. In Kjervick, D; Martinson, L (Eds.) *Women in Health and Illness: Life Experiences and Crisis*. (pp 127-133). W.B. Saunders, Philadelphia.

Valle, S (1981) Interpersonal functioning of alcoholism counsellors and treatment outcome. *Journal of Studies on Alcohol.* V42, pp 783-790.

Waterworth, S (1995) Exploring the value of clinical nursing practice: The practitioners' perspective. *Journal of Advanced Nursing.* V22, pp 13-17.

Watson, J (1985) Watson's philosophy and theory of human caring in nursing. In Rhiel-Sisca, J (Ed.) *Conceptual Models for Nursing Practice* (3rd Ed.). Appleton and Lange, Norwalk, CT.

Wheeler, K; Barret, E (1994) Review and Synthesis of Selected Studies on Teaching Empathy: Implications for Nursing Research and Education. *Nursing Outlook.* V4, pp 230- 236.

Williams, A (1992) Where has all the empathy gone? *Professional Nurse* (Nov), p 134.

Williams, C (1979) Empathic communication and its effect on client outcome. *Issues in Mental Health Nursing.* V2, pp 15-26.

Williams, C (1990) Biopsychosocial elements of empathy: A multidimensional model. *Issues in Mental Health Nursing.* V11, pp 155-174.

Wilson, H; Kneisl, C (1983) *Psychiatric Nursing* (2nd Ed.). Addison- Wesley: Menlo Park, CA.

Wilt, H; Evans, C; Muenchen, R; Guegold, G (1995) Teaching with entertainment films: an empathic focus. *Journal of Psychosocial Nursing.* V33, pp 5 -14.

Wisser, S (1974) Those Darned Principles. *Nursing Forum.* V13, pp 386-392.

Wong, J (1979) The Inability to Transfer Classroom learning to Clinical Nursing Practice: A learning Problem and its Remedial Care. *Journal of Advanced Nursing.* V4, pp 161-168.

Woods, N; Catzanaro, M (1988) *Nursing Research: Theory and Practice.* CV Mosby Co., St Louis.

Zoske, J; Pietrocarlo, D (1983) Dialysis Training Exercises for Improved Staff Awareness. *American Association of Nephrology and Technicians Journal.* pp 19-39.

Appendix 1

The empathy scale and users' guide

Instructions

The instrument contains 12 items that describe behaviours or attitudes of a counsellor (e.g. a nurse) during verbal interaction with his/her client or patient. Read each statement and decide the degree to which you perceive the person that you are rating (e.g. yourself, your nurse helper, or an associate, etc) as like or unlike the statement when applied to a recent relationship. You are asked to give an opinion on every statement according to the following Scale.

1. Always Like (100%)
2. Nearly Always Like (90%)
3. Frequently Like (75%)
4. Quite Often Like (50%)
5. Occasionally Like (25%)
6. Seldom Like (10%)
7. Never Like (0%)

Please read each statement on the empathy instrument and consult the operational definitions and clinical examples (provided in the Users Guidelines) before scoring the instrument. Tick (✓) one response for each item on the scale.

The Items on the Reynolds Empathy Scale

	Always like 100%	Nearly always like 90%	Frequently like 75%	Quite often like 50%	Occasion-ally like 25%	Seldom like 10%	Never like 0%
1. Attempts to explore and clarify feelings							
2. Leads, directs and diverts							
3. Responds to feelings							
4. Ignores verbal and non-verbal commu-nication							
5.Explores personal meaning of feelings							
6.Judgmental and opinionated							
7.Responds to feelings and meanings							
8.Interrupts and seems in a hurry							
9. Provides the client with direction							
10. Fails to focus on solutions/does not answer direct questions /lacks genuineness							
11. Appropriate voice tone, sounds relaxed							
12. Inappropriate voice tone, sounds curt							

ITEM 1

ATTEMPTS TO EXPLORE AND CLARIFY FEELINGS

Operational Definition

Invites the client to describe or evaluate feelings, listens and observes. Useful when the counsellor has no knowledge of the client's world. For that reason, differs qualitatively from item 5. Essentially, the counsellor is inviting the client to clarify the meaning of their communication by providing more detail about their emotional experience.

Clinical Examples

"Tell me how you are feeling now."
        or
"Describe how you feel."

Next, the counsellor waits for a response, noting the client's verbal and non-verbal behaviours and responds to this communication by seeking clarification and/or further information. For example:

"Describe what you mean by depressed" etc. Counsellors should include the feeling word expressed by the client.
        or
"What goes on when you feel depressed?" etc.
        or
"I'm having difficulty understanding exactly what you mean. Could you explain what happens to you some other way so that I can understand better."

If the client is 'blocking', i.e. unable to be open about emotional experiences, or concerns about their health, this problem becomes the 'here and now' issue for the clinical interview. The counsellor will focus on the problem in a manner that allows the client to continue to feel accepted, while able to make choices. For example:

"Are you feeling tense, uncomfortable etc, while talking to me?"
        or
"If talking about... is uncomfortable, tell me a bit about yourself as a person."
        or
"This is your time, talk about anything that you feel is important."
        or
"Talk about what is comfortable to you, at this moment."

ITEM 2

LEADS, DIRECTS AND DIVERTS

Operational Definition

Diverts the client from an area of concern by changing the topic. Generally, this means ignoring the emotional message by concentrating on superficial detail. However, it could also mean that the counsellor totally ignores the client's message and initiates a fresh topic of conversation.

Clinical Examples

Client : *"I used to be in control of my life, made my own decisions, did what I liked. Often I went abroad on the spur of the moment, Switzerland and so on."*

Nurse : *"Tell me about Switzerland."*
        or
Client : *"I've just had the baby, and what with getting over that, this problem with the back passage came out of the 'blue.'"*

Nurse : *"How is the baby?"*
Client : *"Fine."*
Nurse : *"Is it a boy or a girl?"*
Client : *"A girl."*
Nurse : *"Lovely, so you were pleased?"*
Client : *"Yes."*
Nurse : *"Is she good?"*
Client : *"She's really good. She sleeps all night."*
Nurse : *"Who's looking after her today?"*
Client : *"Her Grandma."*
Nurse : *"I bet she's enjoying that?"*
Client : *"Yes."*

Additionally, when diverting clients from areas of concern, counsellors tend to avoid asking about feelings. For example:

Client : *"I don't know what's happening to me."*
Nurse : *"Cheer up, things could be worse."*
        or
        "Oh come on, things are better than they used to be."

ITEM 3

RESPONDS TO FEELINGS

Operational Definition

Verbalises what the client is feeling or attempting to communicate in a manner that allows the clients to confirm or refute the message.

Clinical Examples

"So it sounds as if you're saying...?"
           or
"You are giving me the impression that...?"

When responding to feelings, counsellors should include a feeling word in their attempt to clarify what the client means. For example:

"You sound angry about that?"
           or
"Sounds as if you felt a failure?"
           or
"Sounds as if you were out of control; enraged?"

ITEM 4

IGNORES VERBAL AND NON-VERBAL COMMUNICATION

Operational Definition

Fails to focus on and attempt to clarify the meaning of the client's verbal and non-verbal communication. Differs from Item 2 in that the counsellor fails to explore fully, the client's message, but does not change the topic, or totally ignores the message.

Clinical Examples

Client :   *"I have been very depressed lately, and I didn't really feel hungry. I have only been drinking water rather than taking my diet."*

Nurse : *"They recommended that you drink plenty of water anyway, so that was a good thing. I note on the card that you are a diabetic, so having this diet hasn't caused any problems with that, has it?"*

or

"I feel 'browned' off."

Nurse: *"I know how you feel."*

Often, counsellors fail to notice that verbal and non-verbal communications are not synchronised. For example:

Verbal Behaviours	Non-Verbal Behaviour
Client : *"No this test doesn't worry me at all. I don't worry about anything. If I had to have my legs cut off, then off and be done with it".*	While saying this the client fidgets, avoids eye contact, sounds irritated and displays other physiological reactions such as trembling and sweating.

Nurse : *"That's very good that you are not frightened of anything. Nothing at all."*

ITEM 5

EXPLORES PERSONAL MEANING OF FEELINGS

Operational Definition

Assists client to explore the personal meaning of feelings by recreating significant life experiences that surface in the client's communication. Focus is on the client's, not the therapist's views. Differs from Item 1 because the counsellor attempts to link life events to specific feelings, following some experiential knowledge of the client's world.

Clinical Examples

"So when you say that you feel okay today, how is that in comparison with yesterday morning?"

      or

"Talk about one day at home, and how you felt at that time."

      or

"For instance - describe what went on at that time, when you felt desperate, etc.!"

ITEM 6

JUDGMENTAL AND OPINIONATED

Operational Definition

Expresses value judgments, gives inappropriate advice, advice that is not asked for, or argues with the client.

Clinical Examples

Client : *"I've had a scan (clients starts to cry). I don't know what I'm going to do. I can't stand, I can't do anything."*

Nurse : *"Now, you ARE going to be alright."*

      or

Nurse : *"Do you want to tell me about how you feel?"*

Client : *"No. I'll be all right, it's not that I'm chicken."*

Nurse : *"Well most people are nervous. It's understandable."*

      or

Client : *"It's awful, I feel like a 16 year old kid."*

Nurse : *"You shouldn't feel like that. You have an awful lot of things going for you."*

ITEM 7

RESPONDS TO FEELING AND MEANING

Operational Definition

Attempts to capture and express the client's personal reason for a particular feeling state. Uses a format such as: " YOU FEEL.......BECAUSE......."

Clinical Examples

"You feel anxious because of what your biopsy results might reveal."
        or
"You feel annoyed because you haven't been able to achieve your ideal weight yet."

        The exact words of the formula are not important - they only provide a framework for communicating understanding to the client. Alternative formats include:
"It feels...when..." or "You're feeling...now..." For example:

"It feels lonely when you go to the office, because you don't get respect."
        or
"You're feeling useless now that the family don't need you so much."

ITEM 8

INTERRUPTS AND SEEMS IN A HURRY

Operational Definition

Talks over the client. Talks rapidly. Does not allow time to verbalise, does not listen fully to the client's message.

Clinical Examples

In part this behaviour may be observed through long rambling responses on the part of the counsellor (i.e. responses that are longer than the client's verbalised responses). These long responses may have the effect of further reducing a client's verbalisation. Additionally, the counsellor interrupts clients before they have completed their message, thus failing to accurately hear that message and as a consequence misinterpreting what the client is saying. For example:

Client :   *"I found that one minute I was feeling like I was getting better and the next minute I was back to square 1. I feel..."*
Nurse :   *"It takes about 4-5 days before you start to feel really better, but it will take 6-8 weeks before you actually start getting over it. These things take time, but the first couple of days when you are getting a lot of drugs is when you are most uncomfortable."*

Client :   *"Uhuh."*
         and
Client :   *"I shouldn't have had them (the tablets). I didn't want to. I wish I had
         refused the..."*
Nurse :   *"But did it help the pain?"*
Client :   *"I wasn't in much pain, it was just a spasm."*

ITEM 9

PROVIDES CLIENT WITH DIRECTION

Operational Definition

Assists client to find solution to personal problems in a manner that reflects the
client's preferences.

Clinical Examples

Examples may be viewed in three phases. First step involves helping the client to
explore the effectiveness of current coping strategies. For example, the counsellor
might say:

"What do you hope to happen with the extra medication?"
         or
"When you avoid busy places how do you feel?"
         or
"When you get mad at people, what happens next?"

The next step is to help the client to seek new solutions for personal
problems. For example:

"Can you think of any alternative ways of dealing with these feelings?"
         or
"How else can you get those people to do what you want?"

The ultimate objective of the counsellor is to assist the client to find new
(more effective) solutions to personal problems. Once the counsellor has helped
the client to explore and evaluate potential coping strategies, he/she is in a good
position to know where the client wants to be. The final phase of providing
direction involves making a clarification statement that includes a specific client
problem. The following responses are examples of statements that are high in
direction.

"You feel really 'down' because your boss doesn't communicate with you and you want to ask him what's going on."

The second part of that response, 'and you want', provides the client with direction, it reflects where he wants to be. An alternative format could be: "You want...and you would like to try..." That response also reflects the client's new solutions for problematic situations.

ITEM 10

FAILS TO FOCUS ON SOLUTIONS/DOES NOT ANSWER DIRECT QUESTIONS/LACKS GENUINENESS

Operational Definition

Fails to respond to direct questions, or appears flustered, hesitates, appears lost and/or defensive. Fails to explore the needs of the client by responding in a way that fails to explore the goal of the client, is inaccurate, or acts as a diversion. Ignores problem-solving.

Clinical Examples

Client :
: *(laughs) "It was driving me mad. Other people were coming in and going out so quickly, getting things done, and I was stuck here and they still couldn't figure out what was wrong. You know, I've always had a fear of cancer, wouldn't you if you were in my place?"*

Nurse :
: *"Uh huh (hesitates). It's only natural."*

or

Client :
: *"I get so scared that they are not telling me the whole truth. Do you think that they have found something serious?"*

Nurse :
: *"You need to put that question to Dr ......, but I'm sure there is nothing to worry about."*

ITEM 11

APPROPRIATE VOICE TONE, SOUNDS RELAXED

Operational Definition

Sounds friendly, unhurried, interested and comfortable. Mainly conveyed via sound inflection, but can be enhanced by the form of words used.

Clinical Examples

Client: "Can we talk about..."
Nurse: *"Yes of course. Would you like to take a seat."*
        or
Nurse: *"This is your time, begin anywhere."*

Essentially, determining the degree or extent to which the counsellor-client relationship is free of defensiveness will enable raters to determine the extent to which the operational conditions exist. Non-Threatening voice tones tend to convey warmth (respect) and genuineness (openness) and the existence of these conditions can only be determined by the responses of the client toward the counsellor. This means that the client is able to be open, non-hesitant and/or analytical.

ITEM 12

INAPPROPRIATE VOICE TONE, SOUNDS CURT

Operational Definition

Sounds negative, e.g. unfriendly, hostile and impatient. Alternatively negative responses might be conveyed in more passive forms, e.g. bored, disinterested, distracted and lethargic. Mainly conveyed via sound inflection, but can be enhanced by the form of words used.

Clinical Examples

Client : *"Can we talk?"*
Nurse : *"No. Can't you see I'm busy."*
Nurse : *"I know (yawning) that all this stuff must seem pointless to you, but we must be patient."*

Essentially, item 12 is the reverse of item 11. If the counsellor's tone is perceived by the client to be threatening, a degree of defensiveness will exist in the relationship. The responses of the client are likely to be defensive toward the counsellor. This may consist of mumbling, reduced verbalisation, withdrawal from the counselling relationship, or various forms of mood shifts; anger, anxiety, boredom, etc.

Appendix 2

The internal reliability of items on the empathy scale (Cronbach's Alpha)

ITEM TOTAL STATISTICS

	SCALE MEAN IF ITEM DELETED	SCALE VARIANCE IF ITEM DELETED	CORRECTED ITEM - TOTAL CORRELATION	SQUARED MULTIPLE CORRELATION	ALPHA IF ITEM DELETED
ITEM 1	48.17	66.79	.55	.46	.89
ITEM 2	48.17	62.64	.59	.54	.88
ITEM 3	48.09	63.14	.72	.66	.88
ITEM 4	47.74	65.74	.57	.57	.88
ITEM 5	48.68	62.08	.68	.60	.88
ITEM 6	47.69	65.77	.57	.56	.89
ITEM 7	48.55	63.03	.62	.50	.88
ITEM 8	47.71	64.56	.67	.57	.88
ITEM 9	49.02	64.04	.67	.38	.89
ITEM 10	47.79	67.39	.52	.43	.89
ITEM 11	47.92	64.66	.72	.65	.88
ITEM 12	47.28	66.36	.65	.63	.88

RELIABILITY COEFFICIENTS 12 ITEMS.
ALPHA = .89   STANDARDISED ITEM ALPHA = .90

Appendix 3

The internal discriminations of the empathy scale (phi coefficient)

ITEM 1 Phi	=	.79	ITEM 2	Phi	=	.89
ITEM 3 Phi	=	.87	ITEM 4	Phi	=	1
ITEM 5 Phi	=	.94	ITEM 6	Phi	=	.95
ITEM 7 Phi	=	.87	ITEM 8	Phi	=	.95
ITEM 9 Phi	=	.69	ITEM 10	Phi	=	.88
ITEM 11 Phi	=	.76	ITEM 12	Phi	=	.91

The significance level for these correlation coefficients was $p < .001$.

Appendix 4

Pre- and post-course interview schedules
SEMI STRUCTURED INTERVIEW SCHEDULE
(PRE-COURSE): OPEN QUESTION 1
Describe your reasons for doing the Empathy Module.
Prompts: To be used to focus on certain issues if they don't emerge
from initial open question.

Tick (✓) box
when addressed

a) What made you consider it in the first place? ☐
b) Tell me what you know about the content and purpose of this ☐
module?
c) What knowledge do you hope to gain? ☐
d) Which aspects of your job would you like to become more skilled ☐
at?
e) Describe specific persons that you would like to be more effective ☐
with, interpersonally?

OPEN QUESTION 2
Tell me about your preferred ways of learning.
Prompts: To be used to focus on certain issues if necessary.

a) What works best for you in order to gain knowledge? ☐
b) What do you believe works best for you in order to develop skills ☐
needed to build empathic relationships?
c) Where do you believe empathy is best learned? ☐
d) Describe your views about:
    i) Teacher-centred learning, where the focus is on the teacher's ☐
    experiences
    ii) Student-centred learning, where the focus is on the learner's
    experiences ☐
e) Describe your views about distance learning that involves working
    on your own, at your own pace. ☐
f) Describe your expectations of a Supervisor i.e. a person who will
    be responsible for guiding your course work. ☐
g) Describe the personal attributes that you expect Supervisors to ☐
possess.

OPEN QUESTION 3
Describe circumstances that are likely to interfere with your learning.
Prompts: To be used to focus on certain issues if necessary.

Tick (✓) box
when addressed

a) Describe circumstances that may interfere with your learning ☐
during:
    i) Face-to-face contact with your Supervisor ☐
    ii) Studying at home ☐

iii) Practice in the clinical workplace ☐

iv) College based workshops ☐

b) What are your thoughts and feelings about anticipated barriers to learning? ☐

c) How are you likely to respond to barriers to learning? ☐

d) How effective or ineffective are your coping responses likely to be? ☐

OPEN QUESTION 4

Describe anything else about the empathy module and learning that you feel is important.

SEMI-STRUCTURED INTERVIEW SCHEDULE (POST-COURSE): OPEN QUESTION 1

Describe how adequately your pre-course objectives have been met by this module.

Prompts: To be used to focus on certain issues if they don't emerge from initial question.

Tick (✓) box when addressed

a) Tell me what you have learned about the content and purpose of the empathy module. ☐

b) Talk about what you learned about empathy, i.e. new knowledge. ☐

c) Describe aspects of your job that you have become more skilled at. ☐

d) In respect of your behaviours and attitudes on the empathy scale (items 1-12), what, in your view has changed? ☐

e) Describe your present view of your performance in those relationships which you identified (pre-course) as being ineffective. ☐

OPEN QUESTION 2

Describe the learning experiences that facilitated positive learning outcomes for you.

Prompts: To be used to focus on certain issues if necessary.

Tick (✓) box when addressed

a) Talk about the learning experiences that helped you to gain knowledge. ☐

b) Talk about the learning experiences that helped you to learn ☐

skills necessary for building empathic relationships.
c) Describe your views about the structure and organisation of ☐
your course.
d) Describe your views on student-centred learning. ☐
e) Describe your views about distance learning. ☐
f) Describe how your Supervisor aided your learning. ☐
g) Which learning objectives were assisted by your ☐
Supervisor's contribution.
h) Describe the personal qualities of your Supervisor that ☐
influenced your learning.

OPEN QUESTION 3
Describe any circumstances that interfered with your learning.
Prompts: To be used to focus on certain issues if necessary.

a) Describe circumstances that interfered with gaining ☐
knowledge.
b) Describe circumstances that interfered with your ability to ☐
learn and practise empathy building skills.
c) When your learning was blocked, describe your thoughts ☐
and feelings.
d) Describe the theory component or skill that was blocked. ☐
e) Describe how you coped with interferences to learning. ☐
f) Describe how effective your coping response was. ☐
g) Describe any resources available to help you reduce ☐
interferences to learning.

OPEN QUESTION 4
Describe anything else about the empathy module.

Appendix 5

Evaluation of the circumstances occurring during counselling interviews in the clinical area

DIRECTIONS

During the Professional Studies 1 Module on Interpersonal Skills: Empathy, you will be conducting a series of counselling interviews in the clinical area. Immediately following your fifth counselling interview you are invited to complete this questionnaire. When responding to the 9 questions, please think carefully and answer fully. The more information that you provide, the more effectively the nurse educators will be able to understand the sort of help and support needed by continuing education students during their practical work.

1. Describe the specific aspects of the interview area, such as:

    a) The amount of privacy provided?
    b) Freedom from distractions?
    c) Comfort of furnishings?

2. Describe the staffing levels on the ward/department at the time, in respect of:

    a) The skills mix (ie type of staff on duty)?
    b) How this affected your clinical (counselling) interview?

3. Describe the length of your clinical (counselling) interview in relationship to:

    a) Its planned length?
    b) Its actual length?
    c) Reasons for any variance from planned length?

4. What were you attempting to achieve during your clinical (counselling) interview in respect of:

    a) Understanding your client?

b)　　　Helping your client?
Please be as detailed and specific as possible.

5.　　　What were the problems/needs of your client that you consider to be potentially responsive to the counselling approach that your are using? Please be as detailed and specific as possible.

6.　　　How often had you talked to your client prior to this clinical (counselling) interview, a) formally, ie previous counselling interviews and b) informally, i.e. brief conversations in the ward/department?

	Number of Occasions	Total amount of Time
Formally		
Informally		

Comments

7.　　　Describe how the following factors:

a)　　　Your counselling ability,
b)　　　Your client's behaviour, response to you,
c)　　　Your clinical associates,

affected your ability to achieve your objectives,

i)　　　Prior to (immediately before) your interview, and
ii)　　　During the interview?

8.　　　Describe the extent to which the circumstances described here were similar to all previous interviews.

9.　　　Describe other factors which influenced the content and/or duration of your interview, not covered by the other questions.

Appendix 6

Rationale for questions on the interview and survey method

The pre-course interview

The aim of the pre-course interview schedule was to explore properties that students were bringing into education, and their formative experiences of learning. The schedule included three open questions, and associated prompts (subquestions). The prompts, to be used if necessary, sought to focus the respondent's answers on specific issues that evolved from their responses to the open question. The three open questions were:

Question 1 :   Describe your reasons for doing the empathy course.
Question 2 :   Tell me about your preferred ways of learning.
Question 3 :   Describe circumstances that are likely to interfere with your learning.

The central aim of question 1, and associated prompts, was to explore learners' initial characteristics ie. abilities, knowledge, attitudes and commitment to course work. The prompts associated with question one were:

a) What made you consider the course in the first place?
b) Tell me what you know about the content and purpose of the course.
c) What knowledge do you hope to gain?
d) Which aspects of your job would you like to become more skilled at?
e) Describe specific persons that you would like to be more effective with interpersonally.

The central aim of question 2 was to explore the nurses' attitudes to learning and their preferred learning style. The prompts associated with question 2 were:

a) What works best for you in order to gain knowledge?
b) What do you believe works best for you in order to develop skills needed to build empathic relationships?
c)   Where do you believe empathy is best learned?
d) Describe your views about:

i) Teacher-centred learning, where the focus is on the teacher's experiences.
ii) Student-centred learning, where the focus is on the learner's experiences.

e) Describe your views about distance learning, that involves working on your own, at your own pace.

f) Describe your expectations of a Supervisor, ie a person who will be responsible for guiding your course work.

g) Describe the personal attributes that you expect supervisors to possess.

Question 3 was concerned with students' perceptions about barriers to their learning. It was assumed that this question would provide insight into students' perceptions of what impeded learning. The prompts associated with question three were:

a)   Describe circumstance that may interfere with your learning during:
i) Face-to-face contacts with your supervisor.
ii) Studying from home.
iii) Practice in the clinical workplace.
iv) College based workshops.

b)   What are your thoughts and feelings about anticipated barriers to learning?

c)   How are you likely to respond to barriers to learning?

d)   How effective, or ineffective, are your coping responses likely to be?

The post-course interview

The post-course interview was concerned with students' perception of their empathy education. The post-course interview consisted of three open questions and associated prompts that were intended to generate insight into nurses reasons for considering course components to be effective or ineffective. The questions were:

Question 1 :   Describe how adequately your pre-course objectives have been met by this course.

Question 2 :   Describe the learning experiences that facilitated positive learning outcomes for you.

Question 3 :   Describe any circumstances that interfered with your learning.

The central aim of question 1 was to explore what had been learned as a consequence of the course. The question (and associated prompts) focused the respondents' answers onto theoretical knowledge, attitudes to their job, and ability to help people. The prompts associated with question one were:

a)   Tell me what you have learned about the content and purpose of the empathy course.
b)   Talk about what you learned about empathy, i.e. new knowledge.
c)   Describe aspects of your job that you have become more skilled at.
d)   In respect of your behaviours and attitudes on the empathy scale (items 1-12), what in you view has changed? [1]
e)   Describe your present view of your performance in those relationships which you identified (pre-course) as being ineffective.

The central aim of question 2 was to explore the variables contained within the learning environment. The question and associated prompts sought to focus the respondent's answers on aspects of the course that were considered to be essential conditions for learning. The prompts associated with question 2 were:

a)   Talk about the learning experiences which helped you gain knowledge.
b)   Talk about the learning experiences which helped you to learn skills necessary for building empathic relationships.
c)   Describe your views on the structure and organisation of your course.
d)   Describe your views on student-centered learning.
e)   Describe your views on distance learning.
f)   Describe how your supervisor aided your learning.
g)   Which learning objectives were assisted by your supervisor's contribution?
h)   Describe the personal qualities of your supervisor which influenced your learning.

Question 3 was, like question 2, concerned with variables in the learning environment. However, the aim was to probe circumstances that had impeded or slowed learning. The prompts associated with question three were:

---

[1] The empathy scale referred to is the client-centred measure described in Chapter 4.

a)　Describe circumstances that interfered with gaining knowledge.

b)　Describe the circumstances that interfered with your ability to learn and practise empathy building skills.

c)　When you learning was blocked, describe your thoughts and feelings.

d)　Describe the theory component or skill that was blocked.

e)　Describe how you coped with interferences to learning.

f)　Describe how effective your coping response was.

g)　Describe any resource available to you to help you reduce interferences to learning.

The survey method

It was anticipated that answers to the third research question would by provided be the third question on each interview schedule. However, the question was investigated directly by a context of care questionnaire (see Appendix 5) administered to nurses in an experimental group immediately following clinical work with a client. The clinical work was the fifth supervised clinical interview, in a series of six, which was a component of the empathy course.

The questionnaire consisted of questions which originated from the researcher's past experiences of working with students clinically. Comments made by students suggested that variables occurring during clinical work impacted on their ability to practise their theory of empathic relationships. These included: environmental issues such as privacy; the degree of clinical difficulty presented by clients' and the amount of contact with a client prior to clinical interviews. It was anticipated that these data would identify variables in clinical environments which affect nurses' ability to offer empathy.

Appendix 7

Nurses' attitudes to education

Data reported in this appendix is structured around the initial two questions on the pre-course interview and the first question on the post-course interview.

The first two questions on the pre-course interview were:

Question 1:   Describe your reasons for doing the empathy course.
Question 2:   Tell me about your preferred ways of learning.

Question 1 on the interview schedule elicited two themes and several concepts (see Table 14).

Table 14: Themes relating to students' reasons for doing the course

Theme	No. of times mentioned	No. of concepts within Theme
Students' personal goals	132	53
Prior awareness of course work	34	10

The theme of personal goals generated fifty three concepts. The most frequently mentioned concepts can be examined in Table 15.

Table 15: Concepts relating to students' personal goals

CONCEPTS	NO. OF TIMES MENTIONED
Commitment to personal development	13
Understanding the meaning of the other person's experience	9
Developing new (interpersonal) skills relevant to therapeutic helping	8

The following comments illustrate the concepts listed in Table 15.

"I want to do something new, to learn something different. I've only done RGN, and I really feel that I need more education at this stage of my career."
(commitment to personal development)

"In my clinical area we deal with people with alcohol problems or self-harm injuries such as drug overdose or slashed wrists. I would like to be able to understand the basis (meaning) of those persons' problems and actions."
(understanding the meaning of the other person's experience)

"In my area (psychiatry) clients rely on you to get to the crux of many problems in their lives. Sometimes I experience an inability to understand the concerns of my clients, and to assist them to deal with their illness."
(developing new interpersonal skills)

Question 1 elicited a second theme relating to nurses' awareness of module content, and the learning process. Ten concepts were identified within this theme, but only 1 was mentioned by at least 30% of subjects (See Table 16).

Table 16: Concept relating to prior awareness of course work

CONCEPT	NO. OF TIMES MENTIONED
Uncertainty about course content	16

The concept which was mentioned most frequently (n=16) is illustrated by the following comment:

"To be honest, I don't know much about the course. I assume that it's about relationships with patients and staff."
(uncertainty about course content)

Some nurses (n=5) who were confused about course content were also confused about the meaning of empathy. For example:

"You find the word empathy coming up all the time, but there are very few people who know what it means. I'm not sure myself what it means. I think that it's your ability to communicate with somebody, but I don't know if that's right."

Nurses' preferred ways of learning

Question 2 (of the pre-interview schedule) generated one main theme, and fifty three concepts (See Table 17).

Table 17: Theme relating to students' preferred ways of learning

THEME	NO. OF TIMES MENTIONED	NO. OF CONCEPTS
Effective/ineffective learning	216	53

Twelve concepts were mentioned by at least 30% of subjects (see Table 18).

Table 18: Concepts relating to students' perceptions of effective and ineffective learning

CONCEPTS	NO. OF TIMES MENTIONED
Learning empathy via relationships with significant other persons	16
Learning from peers	13
Combining student and teacher-centred learning	13
Guidance from Supervisor	13
Non-defensive and safe supervisory relationship	12
Access to supervision	11
Credibility of supervisors	11
Reading literature	10
Empathic supervisors	9
Flexible course work	9
Limitations of teacher centred learning	9
Preference for student-centred learning	7

The following comments illustrate the concepts listed in Table 18.

"I suppose that empathy is best learned from practice, working with other people, in the real world."
(Learning empathy via relationships with significant other persons)

"Skills are best learned during application of knowledge during interpersonal relationships with people and observation of other people."
(Learning from peers)

"You learn a lot from your own experience, but it doesn't mean that you are not learning because someone else has taught you. It's a shortcut, you don't have to make your own mistakes, when you learn from other people's mistakes."
(Combining student and teacher-centred learning)

"I don't mind self-assessment, but I prefer to share my learning. I want my supervisor to guide me by identifying things that I hadn't considered. Sometimes I might be on the wrong track, and I need to be guided back."
(Guidance from supervisor)

"You must not feel threatened by a supervisor. If you do, you are likely to feel stupid. You want to feel unthreatened, feel like an equal."
(Non-defensive and safe supervisory relationship)

"You need to have the feeling that they (supervisors) are accessible to you, when you need them, especially when you need to talk about a (learning) crisis."
(Access to supervision)

"I think that the main thing is that supervisors know their subject. You learn a lot from your own experience, but you don't always recognise what you have learned unless you get advice, or direction, from someone else."
(Credibility of supervisors)

"Reading journal articles can help you to gain knowledge about the subject."
(Reading literature)

"The supervisor needs to be an empathic person who understands my fear of not measuring up (clinically) as well as I feel that I should. I need someone who will help me to look at my experiences, and who understands also, the constraints to learning that might be there."
(Empathic supervisors)

"Distance learning appeals to me because you have control over the learning process and can work it around other life commitments. It is flexible."
(Flexible coursework)

"You can get an idea about what is expected from what a teacher tells you, but I don't really think that you can appreciate what a subject is about, unless you experience it for yourself. Who is to say that a teacher's opinion is correct?"
(Limitations of teacher-centred learning)

*"My experiences are so valuable because they are mine. I can relate to
my own experiences because I experienced them."*
(Preference for student-centred learning)

Nurses' perceptions of the outcomes of empathy education

The extent to which nurses perceived that the course was effective in learning how
to offer empathy was probed by Question 1 on the post-course interview. The
question asked, was:

Question 1 : Describe how adequately your pre-course objectives have been
met by this module.

The question elicited five themes and numerous concepts (see Table 19).

Table 19: Themes relating to outcomes of education

THEME	NO. OF TIMES MENTIONED	NO. OF CONCEPTS WITHIN THEME
New attitudes, insights, and skills	126	35
New knowledge	18	8
Therapeutic benefits of empathy	19	13
Academic progress	1	1
Awareness of the purpose of the course	1	1

The theme, which was mentioned most frequently, generated thirty five concepts.
The most common concepts are displayed in Table 20.

Table 20: Concepts relating to new attitudes, insights and skills

CONCEPTS	NO. OF TIMES MENTIONED
Exploring the meaning of feelings and experiences	15
Avoiding diverting or leading	11
Providing direction	10
Awareness of personal limitations	8
Thinking about verbal responses	7
Exploring feelings	7
Reflection on practice	7

The following comments illustrate the concepts listed in Table 20.

> *"I think that I can hear things that I never heard before. When someone verbalises that they are worried, I can recognise the need to explore what lies behind the anxiety and put that to the client. An example would be the anxiety related to chest pain."*
> (Exploring the meaning of feelings and experiences)

> *"My communication skills have improved. I wouldn't just 'shut them off', e.g. when someone is crying. I don't just tap them on the hand and say that I'll come back later, or divert them onto physical things."*
> (Avoiding diverting or leading)

> *"I definitely attempt to help clients to consider available options for coping with their problems, or concerns."*
> (Providing direction)

> *"When I was transcribing my clinical tapes, I found myself to be opinionated and judgmental. I'm trying to stop that, but I need to work on it. I've got to keep reading and practising, otherwise I could lose it."*
> (Awareness of personal limitations)

> *"I feel that I now have more depth to my communication with clients. I put more thought into what I say to them whereas, before the course, I didn't."*
> (Thinking about verbal responses)

> *"I explore and try to clarify feelings now. In the first instance, you respond to feelings, then you start to explore them. Before the course I might have responded to feelings (in an opinionated manner) but no more than that."*
> (Exploring feelings)

"The course makes you look at your own practice closely. It makes you reflect on what you are doing clinically, particularly with clients who face life stressors, such as major surgery, or new learning situations."
(Reflection on practice)

The second theme elicited by Question 1, on the post-course interview, related to new knowledge. This theme, which was mentioned less frequently than attitudes or skills, was mentioned on eighteen occasions, and generated eight concepts. Only one concept was mentioned by at least 30% of nurses and related to knowledge about empathy (see Table 21).

Table 21: Concept relating to new knowledge

CONCEPT	NO. OF TIMES MENTIONED
Acquiring an operational definition of empathy	8

The most frequently mentioned concept related to understanding what empathy meant. Several nurses (n=8) referred to a greater awareness of how the concept could be defined. Examples included:

"Empathy involves being more in touch with the client's feelings. It means putting yourself into the client's position, trying to see what his unmet needs are, rather than the nurse's view of the problem. This involves interrupting less, and providing time for exploration."

The remaining themes elicited by Question 1 did not generate any concepts which were mentioned by at least 30% of the nurses interviewed.

Appendix 8

Effective and ineffective course components

The findings displayed in this appendix were elicited from nurses' responses to Question 2 on the post-course interview. The question was:

Question 2 :   Describe the learning experiences that facilitated positive learning outcomes for you.

This question elicited one main theme and numerous concepts within sub-themes. The number of times that the main theme and each sub-theme was mentioned can be examined in Table 22.

Table 22: Themes/sub-themes relating to students' perceptions of facilitative learning experiences

THEME	SUB THEME	NO. OF TIMES MENTIONED	NO. OF CONCEPTS WITHIN THEME/ SUB THEMES
Course components		230	61
	Supervisory relationship	73	13
	Review of audiotaped clinical work	42	7
	Student-centred focus	33	10
	Self-directed study pack	23	12
	Workshop	21	5
	Distance learning	21	8
	Wider literature review	17	6

The sub-theme of supervision, which related to the general theme of course components, was mentioned more frequently than any other course component (n=73). It generated thirteen concepts, of which four were mentioned by at least 30% of nurses. These concepts can be examined in Table 23.

Table 23: Concepts relating to the supervisory relationship

CONCEPTS	NO. OF TIMES MENTIONED
Open, two-way, non defensive relationship	18
Direction with clinical work	15
Encouragement to reflect on practice	10
Positive reinforcement from feedback	7

The following comments illustrate the concepts listed in Table 23.

"My supervisor was very helpful. We were able to sit and discuss things, including essay drafts, and transcripts of clinical work. I generally knew where I was going wrong, so it helped to say this to her. She was very approachable and honest. If something was 'bad', we were able to discuss it openly."
(Open, two-way, non-defensive relationship)

"My supervisor picked up on clinical issues relating to my responses, e.g. not picking up on a client's anxiety, by concentrating on something that she had said, rather than the expressed problems of the client. She helped me to reflect on the relationship, as 'captured' on tape."
(Direction with clinical work)

"She (the supervisor) encouraged me to reflect on practice, to notice things that I had missed, and encouraged you to take the learning from that experience into your next clinical interview."
(Encouragement to reflect on practice)

"My supervisor gave me positive feedback on my achievements, particularly on the effective aspects of my clinical work."
(Positive reinforcement from feedback)

The sub-theme of audiotaped review of clinical data was identified by all nurses (n=20) as a critical variable in the learning process. This sub-theme generated seven concepts, three of which were mentioned by at least 30% of nurses. These concepts can be examined in Table 24.

Table 24: Concepts relating to review of audiotaped clinical work

CONCEPTS	NO. OF TIMES MENTIONED
Self-judgment of clinical ability by listening to yourself and reviewing transcripts	19
Studying the effect of your communication on the client's response to you	10
Studying the consequences of new (applied) learning during the next clinical interview	7

The following comments illustrate the concepts listed in Table 24.

"Taping interviews made me listen to myself, you can always learn from that. Writing transcripts also helped. Every night I went home and listened to what I had said. You could easily pick out where you were going wrong, e.g. providing too much direction, getting embarrassed by silences, or not exploring. Particularly obvious was an initial attempt to provide my own solutions to client's problems. It was painful, but it was a learning experience."
(Self-judgement of clinical ability by listening to yourself and reviewing transcripts)

"I think that when you were saying things that you didn't mean to come out as they did, you felt awful. When you made helpful responses, e.g. gave clients a chance to express themselves, you noticed that they did open up to you. This method enabled you to study the impact of your language on clients, in terms of them being open to you, or not."
(Studying the effect of your communication on the client's response)

"The best experiences for me (although the worst at the time) were the taping sessions. Once you had done the tapes, and listened to what you had said, you started to improve clinically, especially when you did several interviews with the same client."
(Studying the consequences of new (applied) learning during the next clinical interview)

Within the sub-theme of student-centred focus, ten concepts were identified, two of which were mentioned by at least 30% of nurses (see Table 25).

Table 25: Concepts relating to the student-centred focus of the course

CONCEPTS	NO. OF TIMES MENTIONED
Reflection on experience	7
Meaningful learning that is relevant to your practice	7

The following comments illustrate the concepts listed in Table 25.

"I think that you can go to college and learn a lot of stuff that is irrelevant to your own work. On this course I dealt with real issues that I meet every day. Putting the responsibility onto me, but also giving me support, made me feel comfortable."
(Reflection on experience)

"My aim was to develop skills - so the student-centred focus was valuable. It helped that we were working with real clients, because my aim was also to look at ways of helping the client."
(Meaningful learning that is relevant to your practice)

Within the sub-theme of workshop, five concepts were generated, two of which were mentioned by at least 30% of nurses (see Table 26).

Table 26: Concepts relating to the workshop

CONCEPTS	NO. OF TIMES MENTIONED
Preparing for clinical practice via simulated clinical work	8
Peer support by sharing problems of learning	7

The following comments illustrate the concepts listed in Table 26.

"The simulated practice felt quite natural after a while. Practising some of the skills to be used in clinical practice made me less anxious about the clinical work (that was to follow) with real clients. During clinical work, you need to appear to know what you are doing with the client."
(Preparing for clinical practice via simulated clinical work)

"Peer interaction during the workshop was very supportive. It was nice and relaxed, knowing that you are not the only one 'tearing your hair out'. It is comforting."
(Peer support by sharing problems of learning)

The sub-theme of wider literature review generated six concepts, only one of which was mentioned by 30% of subjects (see Table 27).

Table 27: Concept relating to the wider literature review

CONCEPT	NO. OF TIMES MENTIONED
Extending knowledge of empathy by reading published literature	10

The concept displayed in Table 27 is illustrated by the following comment:

> *"The majority of articles that I read were brilliant. They really did help me understand what a variety of people meant by empathy. There seems to be a diverse thinking and disagreement about the topic."*

Appendix 9

Barriers to empathic behaviour in nurses' clinical environments

The findings displayed in this appendix were elicited from the third question on the pre and post-course interview schedules and the context of care questionnaire. Insight into nurses' anticipation of barriers to empathy in clinical environments resulted from their responses to question 3 of the pre-course interview. The question was:

Question 3 : Describe circumstances that are likely to interfere with your learning.

Question 3 elicited two themes and numerous concepts which related to those themes. The number of times that each theme was mentioned and the frequency of concepts for each theme, can be examined in Table 28:

Table 28: Themes relating to barriers to learning

THEME	NO. OF TIMES MENTIONED	NO. OF CONCEPTS WITHIN THEME
Interferences to learning	103	40
Coping with barriers to learning	61	36

Within the theme of interferences to learning, forty concepts were identified. Only one was mentioned by 30% of subjects (see Table 29).

Table 29: Concept relating to students' perceptions of barriers to learning

CONCEPTS	NO. OF TIMES MENTIONED
Workload	15

The following comment illustrates the concept displayed in Table 29:

"There is a great rush in surgical wards to interview clients as rapidly as possible. Time to sit down with clients for prolonged periods is limited, due to numerous admissions, and so on."
(Workload)

Insight into actual barriers to clinical empathy resulted from the third question on the post-course interview. The question was:

Question 3 :   Describe any circumstance that interfered with your learning.

This question elicited three main themes and numerous concepts (see Table 30).

Table 30: Themes relating to impediments to learning

THEME	NO. OF TIMES MENTIONED	NO. OF CONCEPTS WITHIN THEME
Limitations to knowledge and theory application	83	34
Consequences of limitations (barriers) to learning	28	10
Coping with limitations (barriers) to learning	70	27

The theme of limitations to knowledge and theory application generated thirty four concepts. Concepts mentioned by at least 30% of nurses can be examined in Table 31.

Table 31: Concepts relating to limitations to learning

CONCEPTS	NO. OF TIMES MENTIONED
Clinical problems presented by clients	9
Insufficient time to talk to clients for half an hour due to workload	8

The following comments illustrate the concepts displayed in Table 31.

"The interview with one client was very strained. Normally (outside taping sessions) he was very chatty. However, when I got down to talking about his feelings, he didn't seem ready. I concluded it was the wrong time to use certain interventions. Maybe he didn't want to share his feelings because he was a very private man."
(Clinical problems presented by clients)

"There was little time on duty for talking to clients, in spite of this being an important part of nursing. Usually, there was only one trained nurse on a shift, and you were needed elsewhere. There are so many clients to divide your time between; however, that is not the main problem. There

was administration, doctors' rounds, and expectations of the nurse-in-charge."
(Insufficient time to talk to clients for half an hour due to workload)

The theme of consequences of barriers to learning generated ten concepts, only one of which was mentioned by at least 30% of subjects (see Table 32).

Table 32: Concept relating to consequences of barriers to learning

CONCEPTS	NO. OF TIMES MENTIONED
Tension, resulting from anger and irritations	11

The following comment illustrates the concept displayed in Table 32.

"I felt angry, because this clinical work is supposed to be so important to the aim of individualised care. I felt that nobody cared."

The theme of coping with barriers to learning generated twenty seven concepts, two of which were mentioned by at least 30% of nurses (see Table 33).

Table 33: Concepts relating to coping with barriers to learning

CONCEPTS	NO OF TIMES MENTIONED
Supervisory support	16
Gaining reinforcement from fresh insights and ability in clinical practice	8

The following comments illustrate the concepts displayed in Table 33.

"My fears about course work were resolved within the supervisory relationship. If my supervisor had said that everything I did was hopeless, I would have given up. She was sympathetic, and understood that with part-time education and a full time job, you get tired and can't function after a ten-day shift pattern."
(Supervisory support)

"I found this course interesting because it's about learning a skill that is meaningful to my practice on a day-to-day basis. I got a buzz from discovering things about my client."
(Gaining reinforcement from fresh insights and ability in clinical practice)

Data elicited by each question on the context-of-care questionnaire are displayed next. The findings are displayed in tables constructed from the coding system from the instrument. Selected comments are included to illuminate nurses' perception of circumstances associated with clinical work.

The initial question on the context of care questionnaire was:

1.   Describe the specific aspects of the interview area, such as:
  a)   The amount of privacy provided.
  b)   Freedom from distractions.
  c)   Comfort of furnishings.

Responses relating to the degree of privacy can be examined in Table 34.

Table 34: The amount of privacy provided by the interview area

DESCRIPTION OF CLINICAL ENVIRONMENT	NO. OF TIMES MENTIONED
X = Unspecified	-
1 = Ward sitting room	1
2 = Interview room	1
3 = Private area of the client's home	1
4 = Client's bedside in single room	7
5 = Client's bedside in open ward	3
6 = Client's bedside in occupied bay (six beds)	2
7 = Unoccupied bay	1
8 = General (public) office	1
9 = Utility room e.g. treatment/stock room	1
10 = Semi-private area of open ward	2
11 = Other	-

Nurses (n=20) Total responses (n=20)

Responses relating to freedom from distraction can be examined in Table 35.

Table 35: Nurses' perceptions of distractions in the interview area

DISTRACTIONS	NO. OF TIMES MENTIONED
X = Unspecified	-
1 = freedom from distractions	8
2 = Background noise	6
3 = Problems with tape-recorder malfunctioning	1
4 = Interrupted by visitors	1
5 = Interrupted by clinical staff	3
6 = Interrupted by other clients	1
7 = Interrupted by domestic	-
8 = Pressure of time	1
9 = Telephone	1

Nurses (n=20) Total responses (n=20)

Responses relating to comfort of furnishings can be examined in Table 36.

Table 36: Comfort of furnishings in the interview area

COMFORT OF FURNISHINGS	NO. OF TIMES MENTIONED
X = Unspecified	4
1 = Comfortable	9
2 = Reasonable	3
3 = Uncomfortable	4
4 = Other	-

Nurses (n=20) Total responses (n=20)

The following comments illustrate specific barriers to offering empathy in clinical areas:

> *"Although we closed the screens, I didn't feel we had enough privacy to relax."*

(Lack of privacy)

> *"A visiting district nurse's voice was very audible and quizzical. She was having a conversation about why the screens were drawn. She completely blotted out our voices on the taped record of the interview."*

(Distraction in the interview area)

> *"Furnishings were nothing to 'write home' about. It consisted of typical desk and hardback chairs. Paperwork and files were strewn around the office."*
> (Uncomfortable furnishings)

The second question on the context of care questionnaire was:

2.   Describe the staffing levels on the ward/ department at the time, in respect of:

a)   The skills mix (i.e. type of staff on duty).
b)   How this affected your clinical (counselling) interview.

Responses relating to the skills mix can be examined in Table 37.

Table 37: Nurses' responses to the question about skills mix

SKILLS MIX	NO. OF TIMES MENTIONED
X = Not applicable/relevant	9
1 = Sufficient	4
2 = Insufficient	7
3 = In charge (only RN)	5
4 = In charge (not only RN)	4
5 = Not in charge (not only RN)	2
6 = Only nurse (community visit)	1
7 = Supernumerary	2
8 = Chose to interview in own time	6
9 = Other	-

Nurses (n=20) Total responses (n=40)

Responses relating to the effect of the skills mix on the fifth clinical interview can be examined in Table 38.

Table 38: Effect of the skills mix on the fifth clinical interview

EFFECTS OF SKILLS MIX	NO. OF TIMES MENTIONED
X = No comment	1
1 = Not affected	8
2 = Interruptions	4
3 = Restriction to time available	2
4 = Postponement of interview	1
5 = Relaxed	12
6 = Unrelaxed	7
7 = Necessitated interviewing when off duty	6
8 = Other	-

Nurses (n=20) Total responses (n=41)

The following comments illustrate issues relating to skills mix in clinical areas.

> *"The time was picked so that there were no babies due to be fed, and the 'bank' nurse could supervise them and deal with any admissions. She also had the F grade who was in charge, to call on, leaving me free. I did not feel rushed or guilty during the interview."*
> (Consequence of adequate skills mix)

> *"My concentration was not what was desired. I felt under pressure all of the time, because I was listening for crises that can arise (on the ward). I was not as relaxed as I would like to have been."*
> (Consequence of inadequate skills mix)

The third question on the context of care questionnaire was:

3.   Describe the length of your clinical (counselling) interview in relationship to:

   a)   its planned length
   b)   its actual length
   c)   reasons for any variance from planned length

Responses relating to variation in the planned (thirty minute) clinical interview can be examined in Table 39.

Table 39: Variation in the planned length of the fifth counselling interview

VARIATION IN LENGTH OF INTERVIEW FROM PRESCRIBED TIME	NO. OF TIMES MENTIONED
X = No variation	3
1 = More than 10 minutes less	2
2 = 5-10 minutes less	8
3 = 5-10 minutes more	5
4 = 10-20 minutes more	2

Nurses (n=20) Total responses (n=20)

Responses relating to the reasons for variation in the planned length of the fifth clinical interview can be examined in Table 40.

Table 40: Reasons for variation in the planned length of the fifth counselling interview

REASONS FOR VARIANCE	NO. OF TIMES MENTIONED
X = No particular reason	1
1 = Difficulty in conducting interview	4
2 = Did not want to rush	1
3 = Planned length too long for client	3
4 = Inexperience of the nurse	2
5 = Interruptions	4
6 = Client chose to end interview	2
7 = Other	-

Nurses (n=20) Total responses (n=20)

The following comments illustrate issues relating to variations in the planned length of clinical interviews.

"The client was sometimes a bit confused, and tended to start wandering after about 15-20 minutes. She actually said that she felt tired, and that she wanted to shop."

(Planned length too long for the client)

"My greatest difficulty was in finishing on time. My client would start talking at length about something, and I felt that I had to wait until she had finished before saying, 'Maybe this is something that you would like to talk about next time'."
(Inexperience of the nurse)

The fourth question on the context of care questionnaire was:

4. What were you attempting to achieve during your clinical (counselling) interview in respect of:
5.
    a)   understanding your client;
    b)   helping your client.

Responses relating to understanding the client can be examined in Table 41.

Table 41: Nurses' objectives in relation to understanding their client

UNDERSTANDING	NO. OF TIMES MENTIONED
1 = Understand client's worries, fears, problems	6
2 = Explore client's thoughts and feelings	10
3 = Explore effect of clients' past experiences on the present situation	1
4 = Understand the client's perception of illness/treatment	5
5 = Understand the client's health needs	1
6 = Obtain the client's trust	3
7 = Understand clients' coping strategies	3
8 = Other	5

Nurses (n=20) Total responses (n=34)

Responses relating to helping the client can be examined in Table 42.

Table 42: Nurses' objectives in relation to helping their client

HELPING	NO. OF TIMES MENTIONED
X = Not specified	3
1 = Help client cope with client role/ situation	1
2 = Help client find solutions to their problems	6
3 = Encourage verbalization of client's feelings	8
4 = Help client understand their own feelings	1
5 = Help client prepare for discharge	1
6 = Enable client to verbalise concerns	2
7 = Assist client to help themselves	3
8 =Ssupport by providing time exclusive to the client	1
9 = Other	1

Nurses (n=20) Total responses (n=27)

The following comments illustrate nurses' perception of their objectives during clinical interviews.

> *"I wanted to understand the client's reasons for wishing to remain in the hospice, even though her condition would have allowed her to go home for a period.*
> (Explore client's thoughts and feelings)

> *"I hoped that I could assist my client to resolve her problems, without offering direct guidance (my advice)."*
> (Assist client to help themselves)

The fifth question on the context of care questionnaire was:

5.   What were the problems/needs of your client which you consider to be potentially responsive to the counselling approach which you were using?

Responses relating to problems of clients can be examined in Table 43.

Table 43: Clinical problems identified by nurses

PROBLEMS	NO. OF TIMES MENTIONED
X = Not specified	1
1 = Loneliness	3
2 = Guilt	3
3 = Inadequacy	4
4 = Grief	2
5 = Low-self esteem	3
6 = Lack of self confidence	4
7 = Anger	4
8 = Unhappiness/depression	2
9 = Fear/anxiety/panic	4
10 = Bitterness/resentment	1
11 = Alienation	4
12 = Denial	4
13 = Difficulty in coping	5
14 = Obsessional beliefs/behaviours	2
15 = Financial/domestic problems	2
16 = Other	-

Nurses (n=20) Total responses (n=48)

Nurses' perceptions of the needs of clients can be examined in Table 44.

Table 44: Nurses' perception of the clients' needs

NEEDS	NO. OF TIMES MENTIONED
X = Not specified	3
1 = Need to verbalise feelings	6
2 = Need of someone to listen	5
3 = Reassurance	2
4 = Understanding/acceptance	3
5 = Need to find own solutions to problems	3
6= Increase perception of self	2
7 = Need for assertive skills	3
8 = Other	-

Nurses (n=20) Total responses (n=27)

The following comments illustrate nurses' perception of clients problems and needs.

> *"I found that the client was able to tell me about some of his feelings, e.g. guilt and low self-esteem. He normally keeps very guarded, denies the existence of such feelings, choosing to hide behind complaints of physical problems, e.g. 'this pain in my head'."*
> (Clinical problems of the client)

> *"His needs are to make decisions for himself. He feels that he needs to learn how to challenge the establishment (assertion), in order to get the answers that he requires."*
> (Needs of the client)

The sixth question on the context of care questionnaire was:

6.   How often had you talked to your client prior to this clinical (counselling) interview?

a) formally, i.e. previous counselling interview.
b) informally, i.e. brief conversations.

Nurses' previous counselling experience of their client, prior to their fifth clinical interview, can be examined in Tables 45 and 46.

Table 45: Previous formal counselling interviews with the client

NO. OF PREVIOUS INTERVIEWS	NO. OF TIMES MENTIONED
0	6
1	2
2	2
3	1
4	9

Nurses (n=20) Total responses (n=20)

Table 46: Total amount of prior counselling work conducted with the client

TOTAL	NO. OF TIMES MENTIONED
X = No previous counselling	6
1 = Less than 1/2 hour	2
2 = Less than 1 hour	0
3 = More than 1 hour	2
4 = Two hours*	5
5 = More than two hours	5

Nurses (n=20) Total responses (n=20)
* Prescribed amount of counselling time for 4 interviews.

Nurses' informal contacts with their client prior to their formal clinical interview can be examined in Table 47.

Table 47: Number of informal contacts with the client prior to the fifth clinical interview

TOTAL CONTACTS	NO. OF TIMES MENTIONED
0	3
1	2
2	1
3	1
4	1
5	1
Too frequent to count	10
Not specified	1

Nurses (n=20) Total responses (n=20)

The brief nature of informed contracts with clients is illustrated by the following comment:

"I didn't really think much about the client, prior to the interview. When considering the situation, I found that I had spent very little time with the client before the interview. Contacts consisted of many brief conversations while carrying out nursing activities, and small conversations, throughout the day."

Nurses' perceptions of informal contacts can be examined in Table 48.

Table 48: Comments relating to prior informal experience of the client

COMMENTS	NO. OF TIMES MENTIONED
X = None given	4
1 = Little opportunity for previous counselling	2
2 = Spent little time with client before interview	5
3 = Informal contact related to explaining procedures	2
4 = Physical illness dictates conversation	1
5 = Brief conversations in the passing	3
6 = Spent a lot of (informal) time with client	6
7 = Would have liked more time with client	1
8 = Other	0

Nurses (n=20) Total responses (n=24)

The seventh question on the context of care questionnaire was:

7.   Describe how the following factors:

a) your counselling ability;
b) your client's behaviour, or response to you;
c) your clinical associates;

affected your ability to achieve your objectives,

i)   prior to (immediately before) your interview
ii) during the interview.

Responses relating to pre-interview variables can be examined in Table 49.

Table 49: Nurses' perception of pre-interview variables

PRIOR TO INTERVIEW	NO. OF TIMES MENTIONED
1 = Limited counselling ability	5
2 = Inexperience	4
3 = Lack of confidence	3
4 = Nervousness	8
5 = Little contact with client, prior to interview	3
6 = A lot of contact with the client prior to interview	1
7 = Gained confidence through the module	1
8 = Confident	1
9 = Client readily complied	3
10 = Staff supportive	4
11 = Staff unsupportive	6

Nurses (n=20) Total responses (n=39)

Responses relating to nurses perception of their ability during the fifth clinical interview can be examined in Table 50.

Table 50: Nurses' perception of their ability and its impact on the counselling interview

ABILITY	NO. OF TIMES MENTIONED
1 = Inexperienced/room for improvement	10
2 = Lack of confidence	3
3 = Nervousness, which communicated to the client	1
4 = Difficulty enabling client to comprehend purpose/aim of interview	1
5 = Confidence increased	4
6 = Improvement in technique noticed	6
7 = Earlier feedback from supervisor applied to this interview	2
8 = Able to achieve some objectives set	9
9 = No objectives set	1

Nurses (n=20) Total responses (n=37)

Nurses' perception of pre-interview variables and their counselling ability are illustrated by the following comments:

"Before the interview I had to participate in a rescheduled ward round which was 4 1/2 hours late. I wasn't the primary nurse for any of the clients being discussed, and this was holding back my interview, and increasing my nervousness. I felt unsupported."
(Pre-interview variables)

"I have very little practice in counselling, and found that I felt nervous prior to interviews. After I said something to the client I found myself getting flustered, because I felt that I was explaining what I wanted wrongly."
(Perception of ability)

Nurses' perception of the effect of the clients behaviour on the clinical interview can be examined in Table 51.

Table 51: Nurses' perception of clients' behaviour and its effect on the counselling interview

CLIENTS' INFLUENCE ON COUNSELLING	NO. OF TIMES MENTIONED
1 = Lack of trust by the client	2
2 = Lack of understanding of the client's questions	1
3 = Difficulty in understanding the client	1
4 = Client had difficulty in relating to the nurse	1
5 = Client had difficulty in examining feelings	4
6 = Client changed subject often	1
7 = Client found tape-recorder a barrier	1
8 = Client tried to keep the conversation going	4
9 = Relationship building necessary	1
10 = Had trusting relationship with the client	5
11 = Responsive/co-operative client	9
12 = Client appreciated opportunity to talk	5
13 = Obtained insight into client's feelings	5

Nurses (n=20) Total responses (n=40)

The effects of clinical associates on the clinical interview can be examined in Table 52.

Table 52: Effects of clinical associates on the counselling interview

STAFF INFLUENCE	NO. OF TIMES MENTIONED
X = No effect	8*
1 = Unco-operative/uninterested staff	7
2 = Staff of little help	3
3 = Co-operative/supportive/ interested staff	2

Nurses (n=20) Total responses (n=20)

Nurses' perception of the negative affect of clinical associates on their counselling ability is illustrated by the following comment:

> *"My colleagues were tolerant of my counselling work because permission has been granted from 'above'. However, they were not respectful of our need for privacy (i.e. coming behind the screens to hand out oral medications - standing outside the screens and listening)."*

The final two questions on the context-of-care questionnaire were:

8. Describe the extent to which circumstances described here were similar to all previous interviews.
9. Can you think of any other factors or issues that influenced the content and/or duration of your interview?

Responses to Question 8 indicated that 50% of nurses' perceived the circumstances of the interview to be very similar to all previous interviews. The remaining 50% of nurses reported either improved circumstances during the fifth clinical interview, or less favourable conditions than on previous occasions. The final question did not elicit any new variables.

Appendix 10

Content of the self-directed study pack

i)   What We Mean by Empathy.
      a)   Introduction to a New Empathy Scale.

ii)   The Therapeutic Significance of Empathy.
      a)   What we mean by the helping relationship.
      b)   When we can provide helpful interpersonal experiences for clients.
      c)   The relationship of empathy to warmth and genuineness.
      d)   The research evidence relating to empathy.

iii)   Empathy During the Initial Phase of the Helping Relationship.
      a)   Orientating yourself to the client.
      b)   Verbal strategies during the initial phase of the helping relationship.
      c)   Closed and open questions.
      d)   Non-verbal strategies when the client finds verbalisation difficult.

iv)   Empathy During the Working Phase of the Helping Relationship.
      a)   Observing and listening to your client.
      b)   Exploring feelings.
      c)   Self-awareness.
      d)   Responding to feelings.
      e)   Exploring personal meaning.
      f)   Accurate reflection of feelings and thoughts.
      g)   Practising feelings words.
      h)   Responding to feeling and meaning.
      i)   Responding on a regular basis.
      j)   Focusing on the client's message and seeking clarification.
      k)   Providing your client with direction.

v)   Empathy During the Termination Phase of the Helping Relationship.
      a)   Problems associated with termination.
      b)   Preparing your client for termination of the helping relationship.

vi)   Application of Rogerian Constructs to the Counselling Interview.
      a)   Introduction to workshop activity.
      b)   Introduction to clinical activity.

Appendix 11

The initial activity in the self-directed study pack

ACTIVITY 1.1

For your first activity in this study pack, we want you to describe a person or associate who, in your view, recently displayed high or low levels of empathy toward someone that they were attempting to help.

Now discuss your description with your supervisor, and defend the basis for your assumptions.

Index